My Beloved Sophia

HEALING WITH ROSES
COLORING BOOK

I0446863

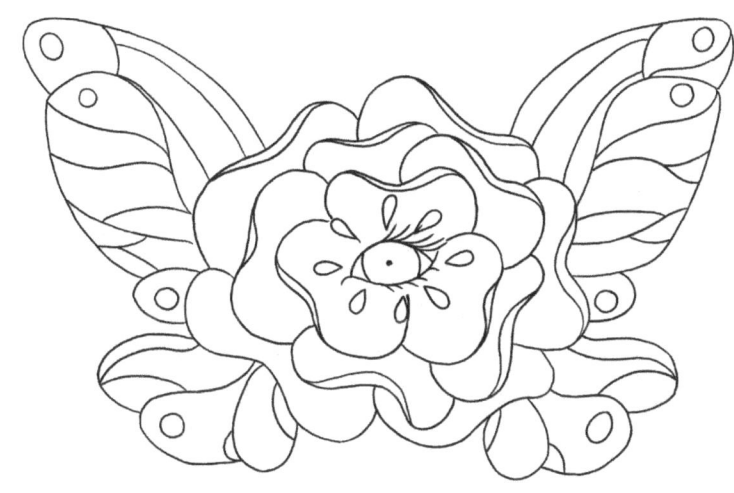

Created and Illustrated By
Isis Escobar Salcedo

Dedication

This book is dedicated to all the beautiful women in my life, starting with my beautiful mother, the brave soul that brought me into this world. To my beloved grandmothers, wise ancestors, aunts, friends, spiritual guides and teachers. For all the beautiful guidance and amazing examples that have helped me find myself.

A very sweet thanks to Maria Luisa Aviles Lucero lovingly known as "La Bicha" for showing me that coloring is so much fun.

This book is also a dedication to all the Divine Masculines in my life, those who are brave enough to love unconditionally and heal the sadness from those that are not able to.

Thank you all who come In contact with this book, may the Sacred Rose, Divine Mother, Divine Feminine, bloom in your hearts and nourished the beautiful smile of our children, the future of our world.

Love Always,

Isis Escobar Salcedo

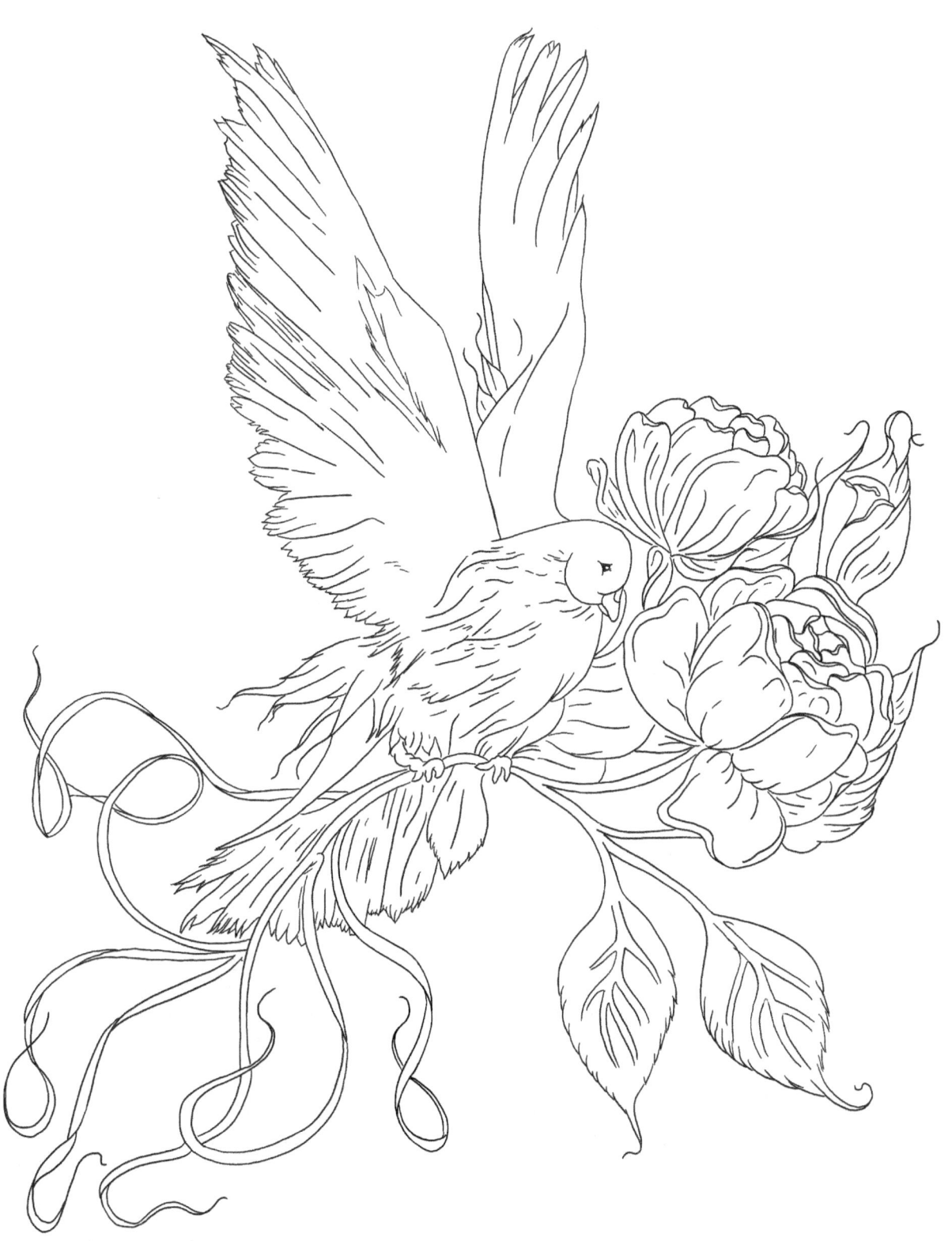

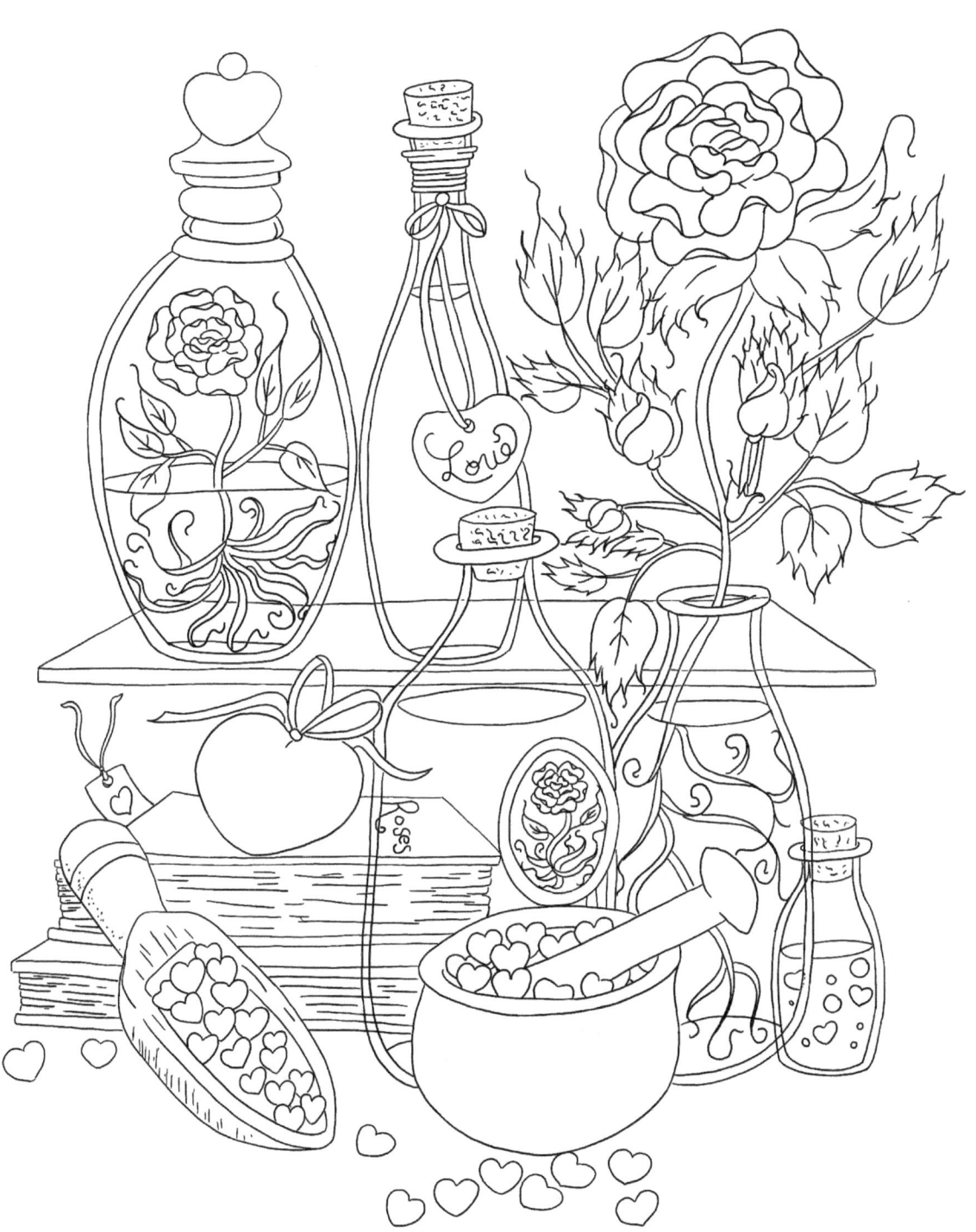

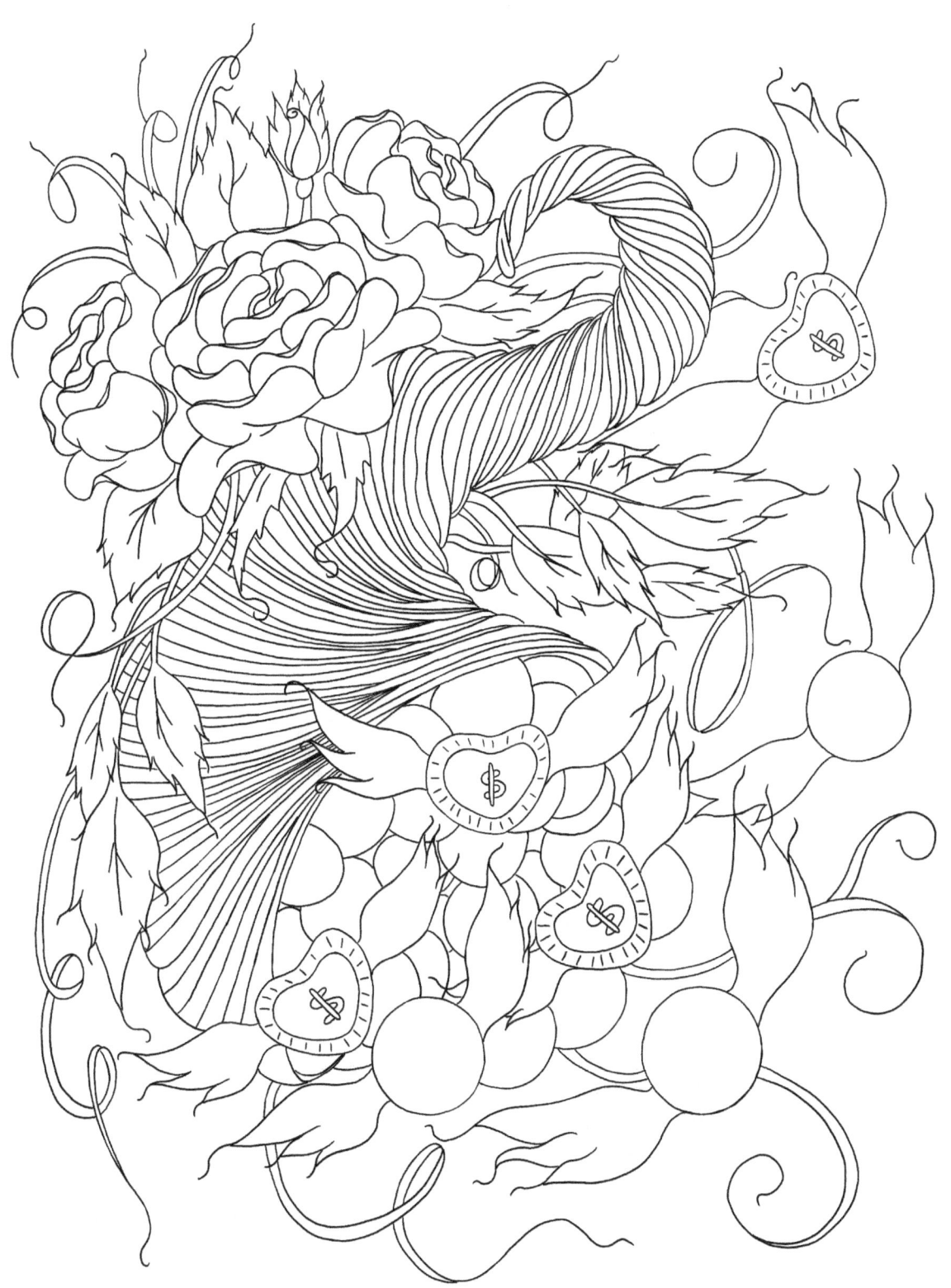

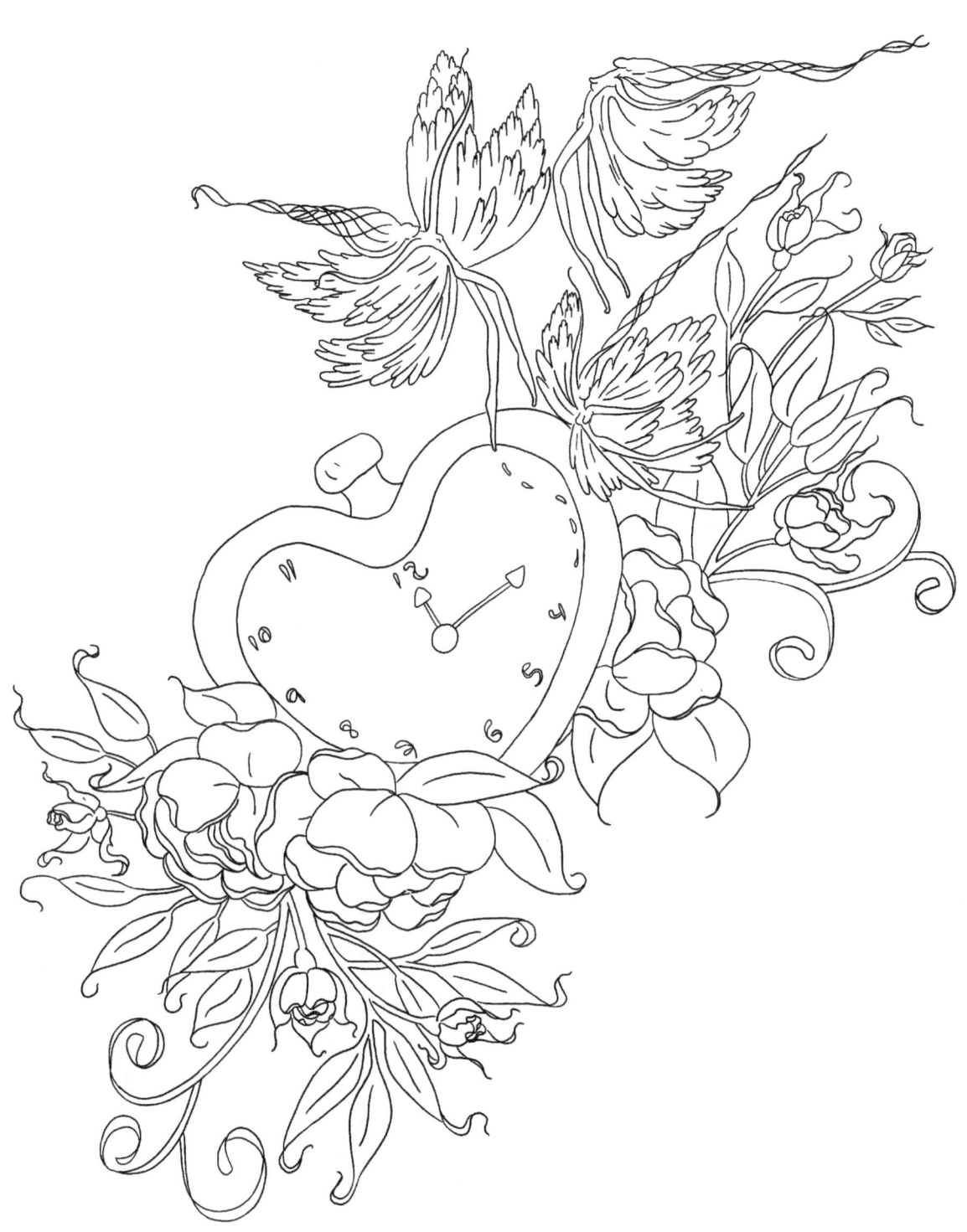

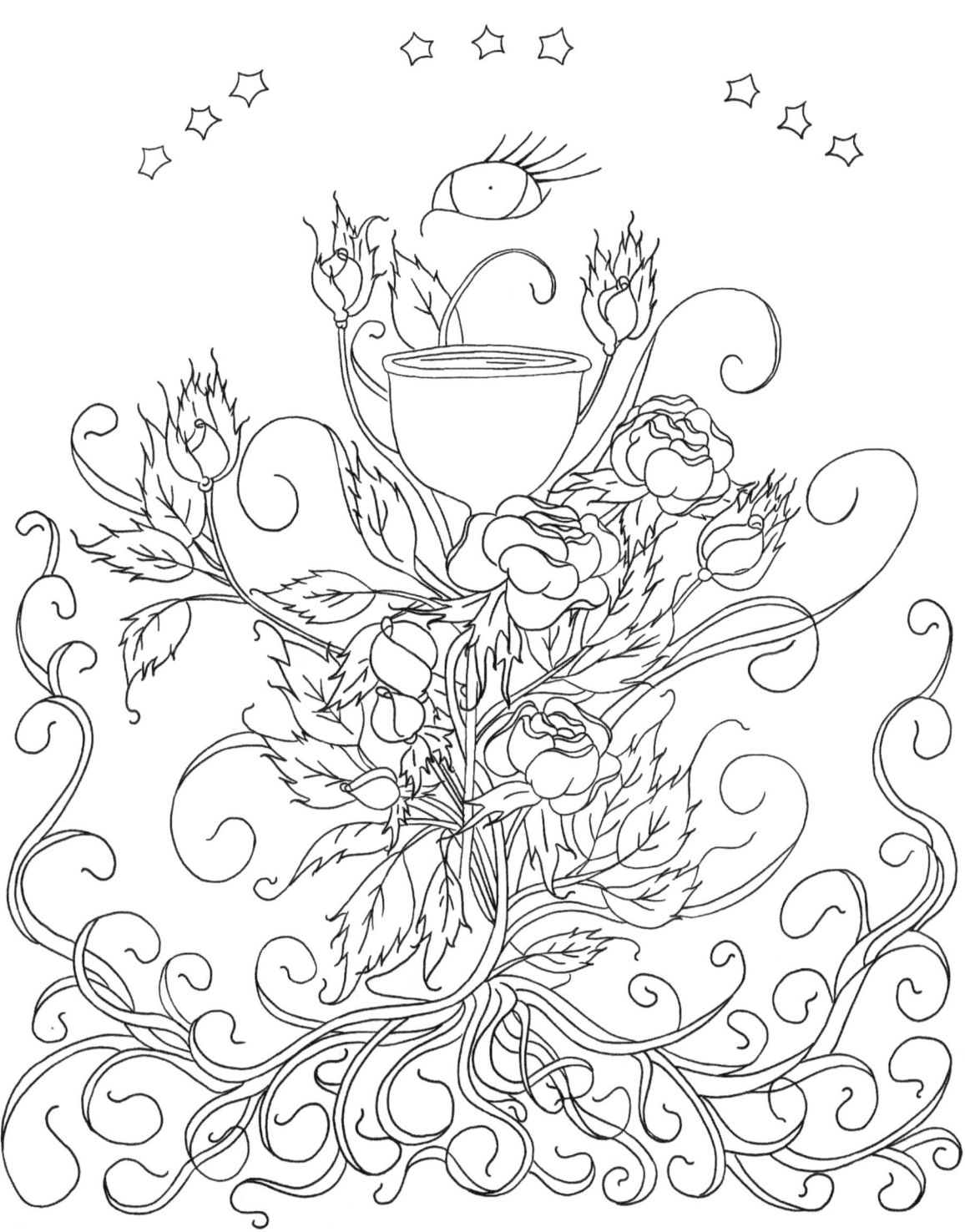

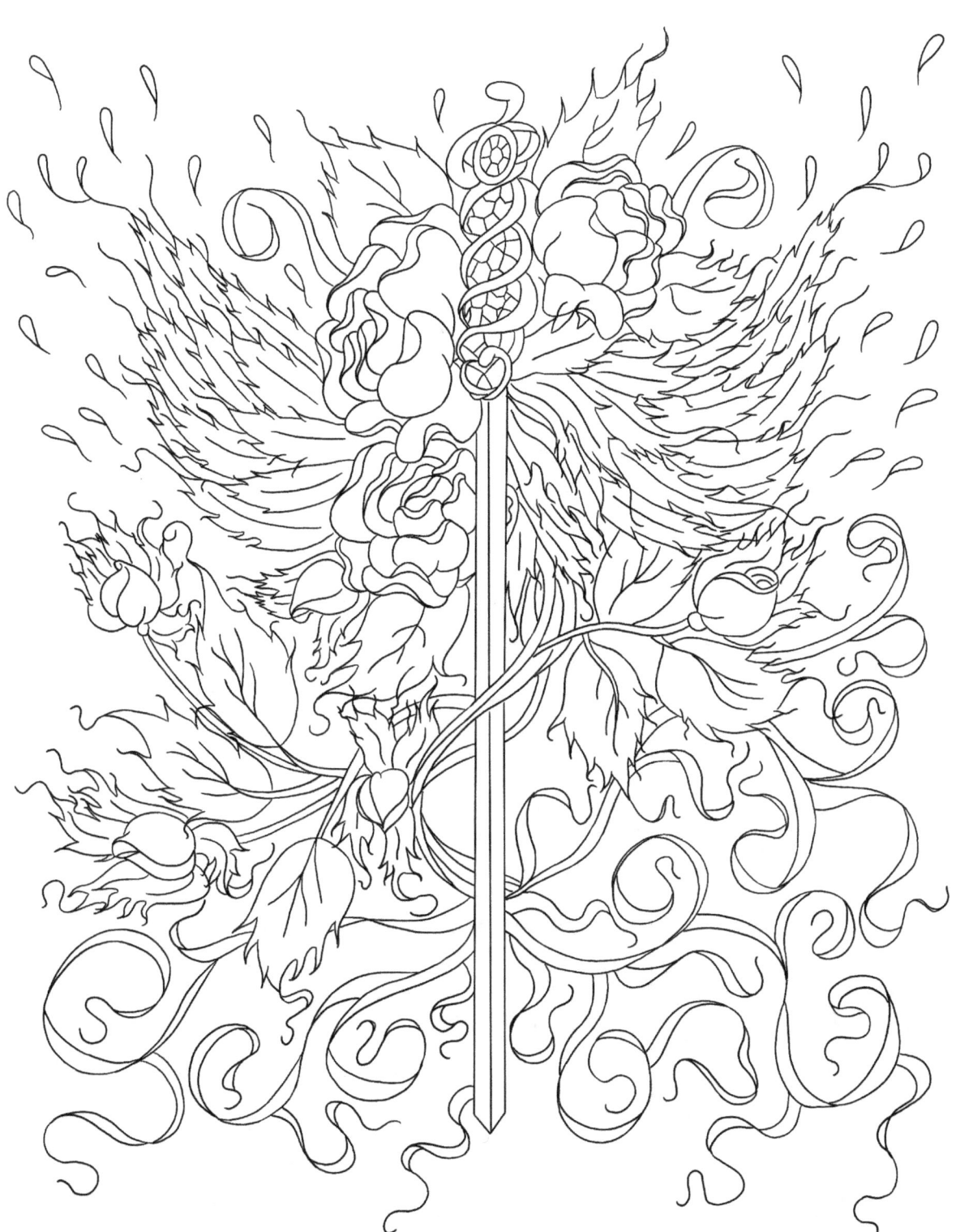

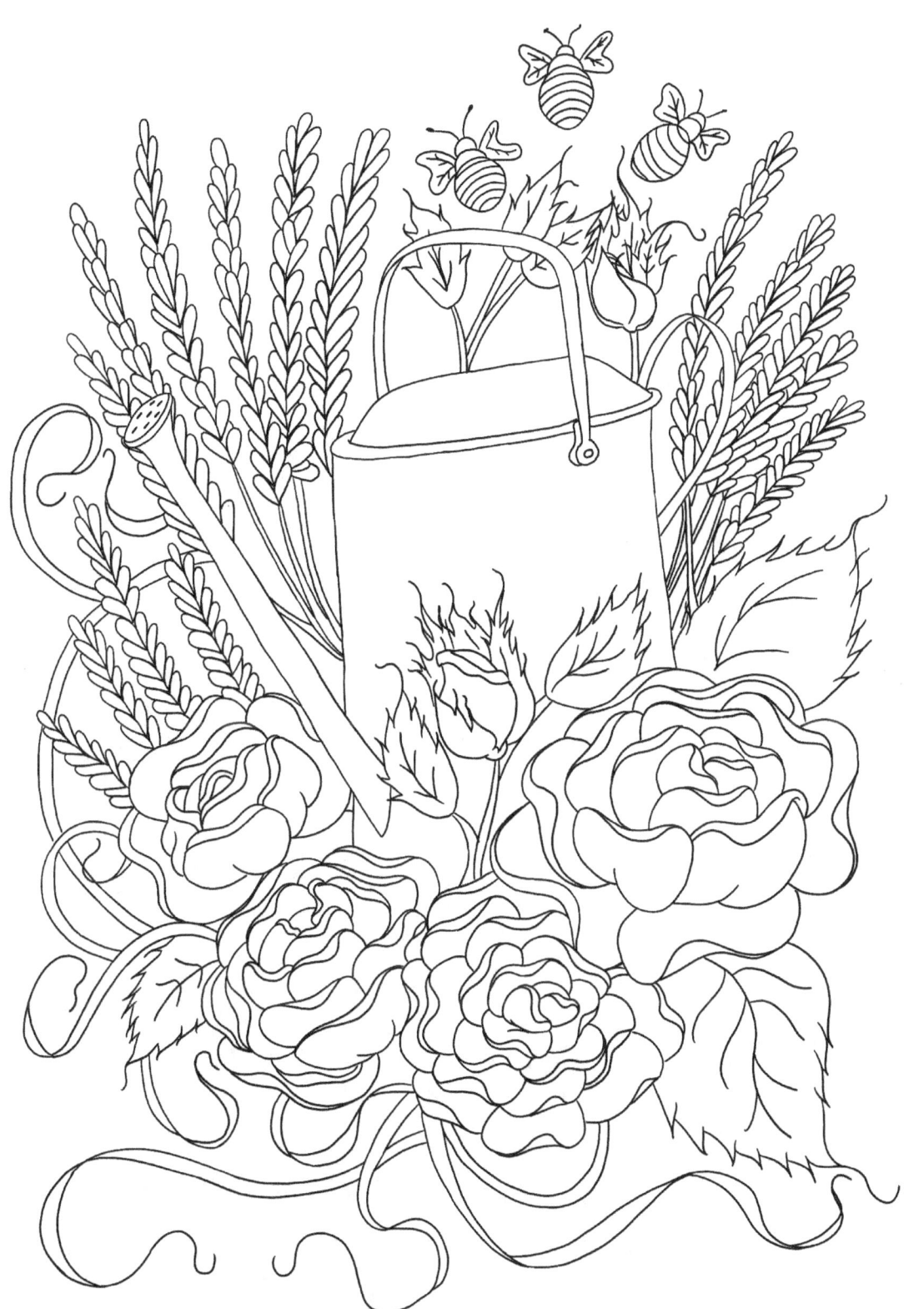

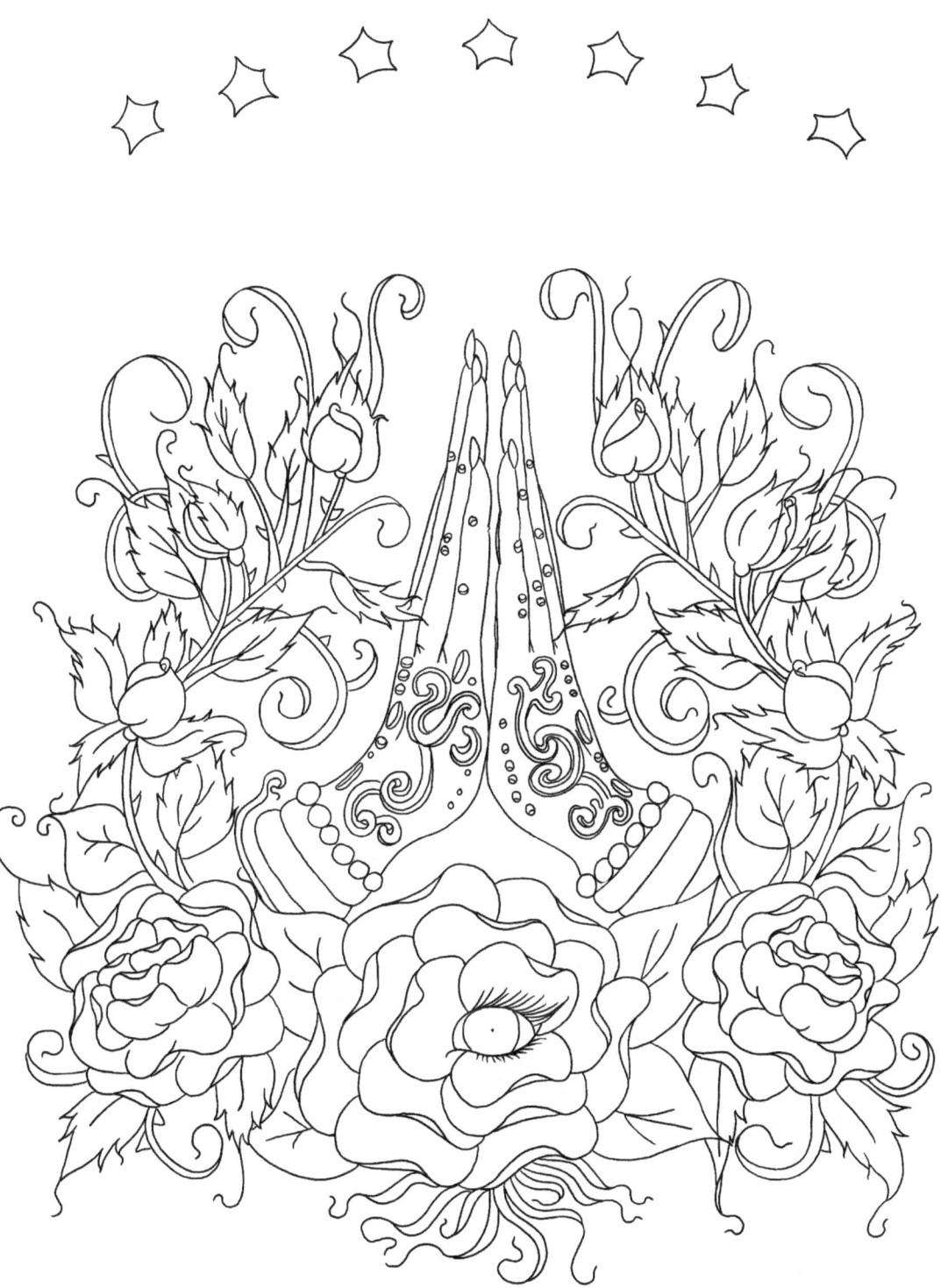

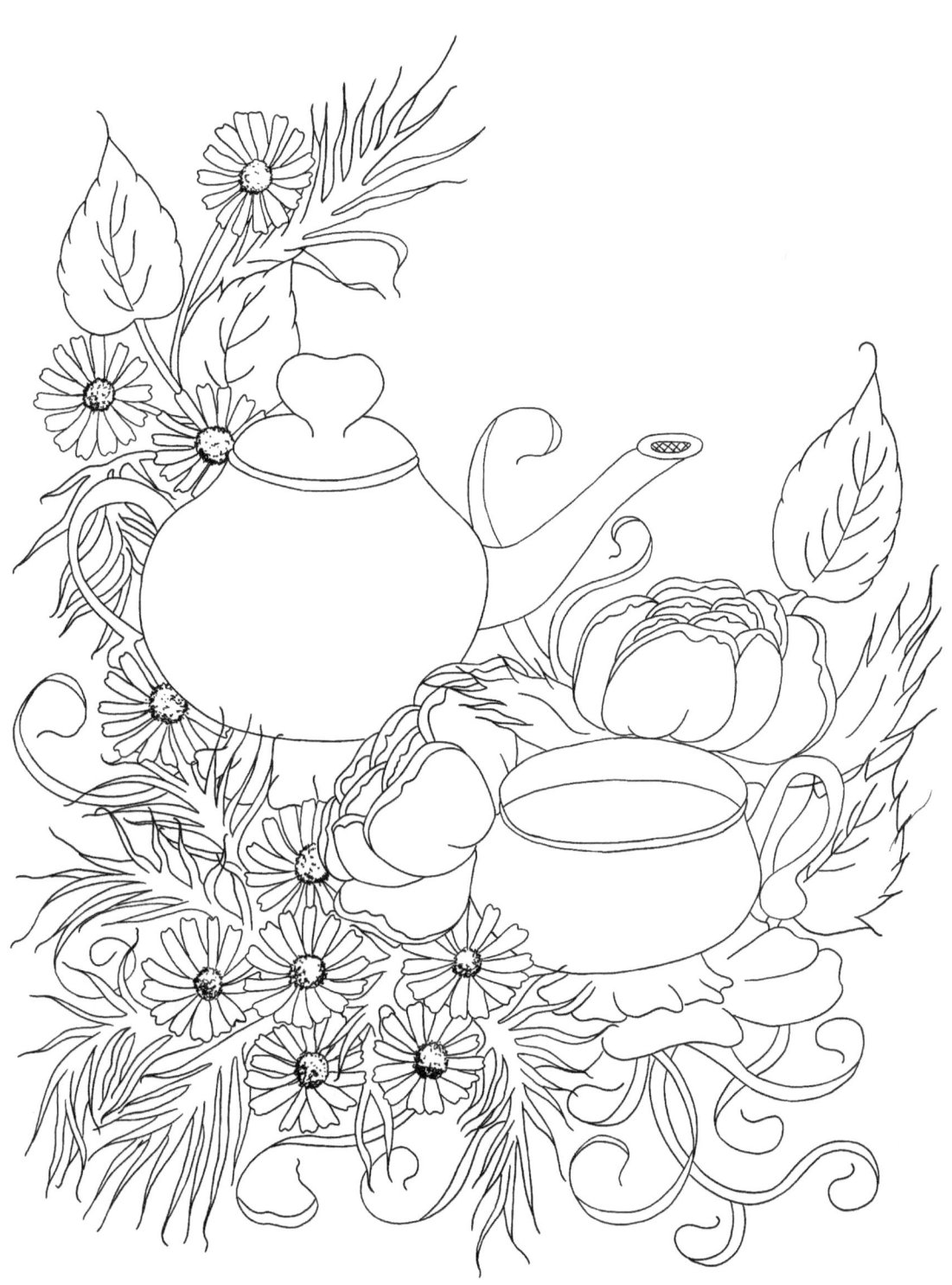

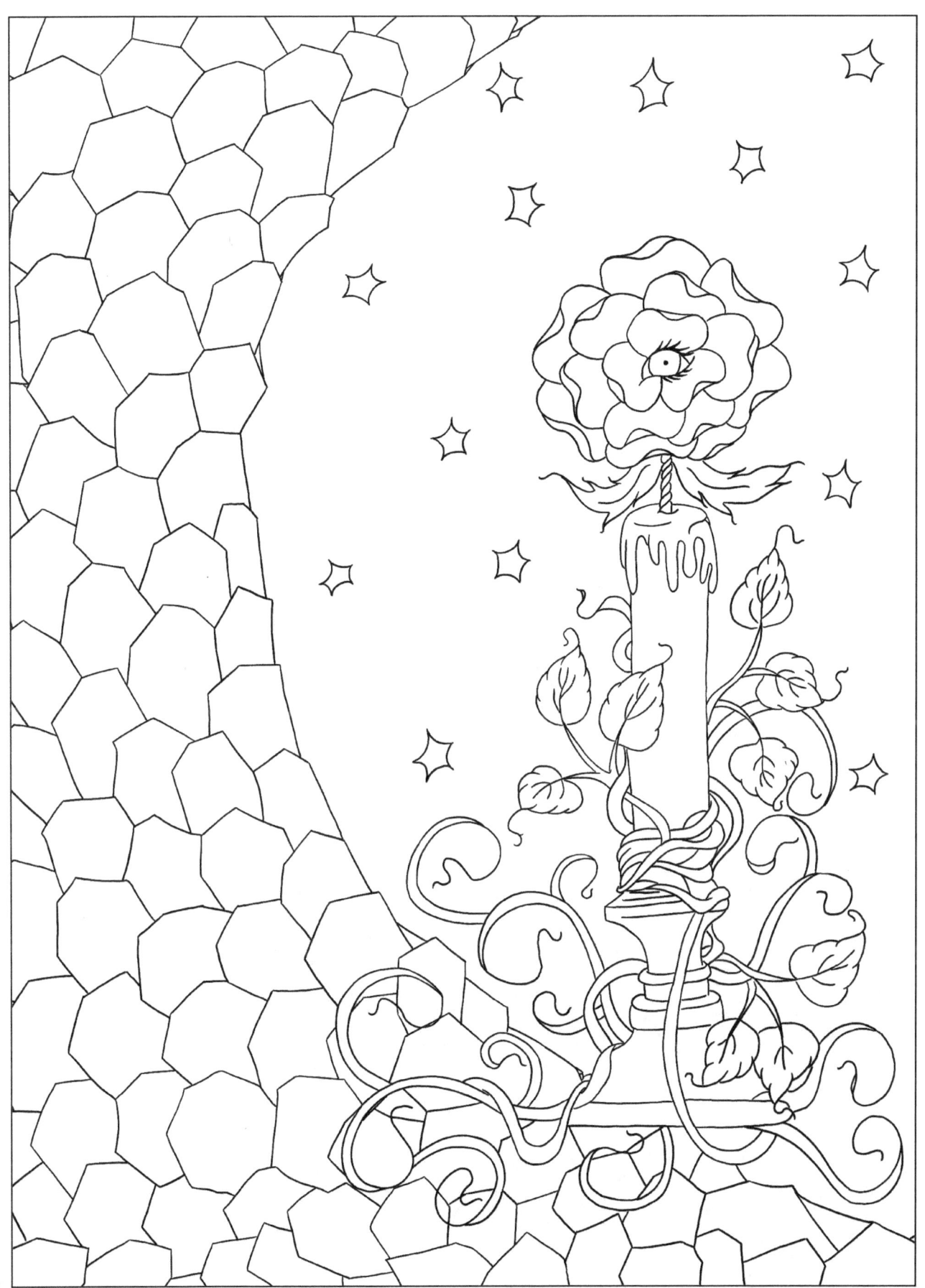

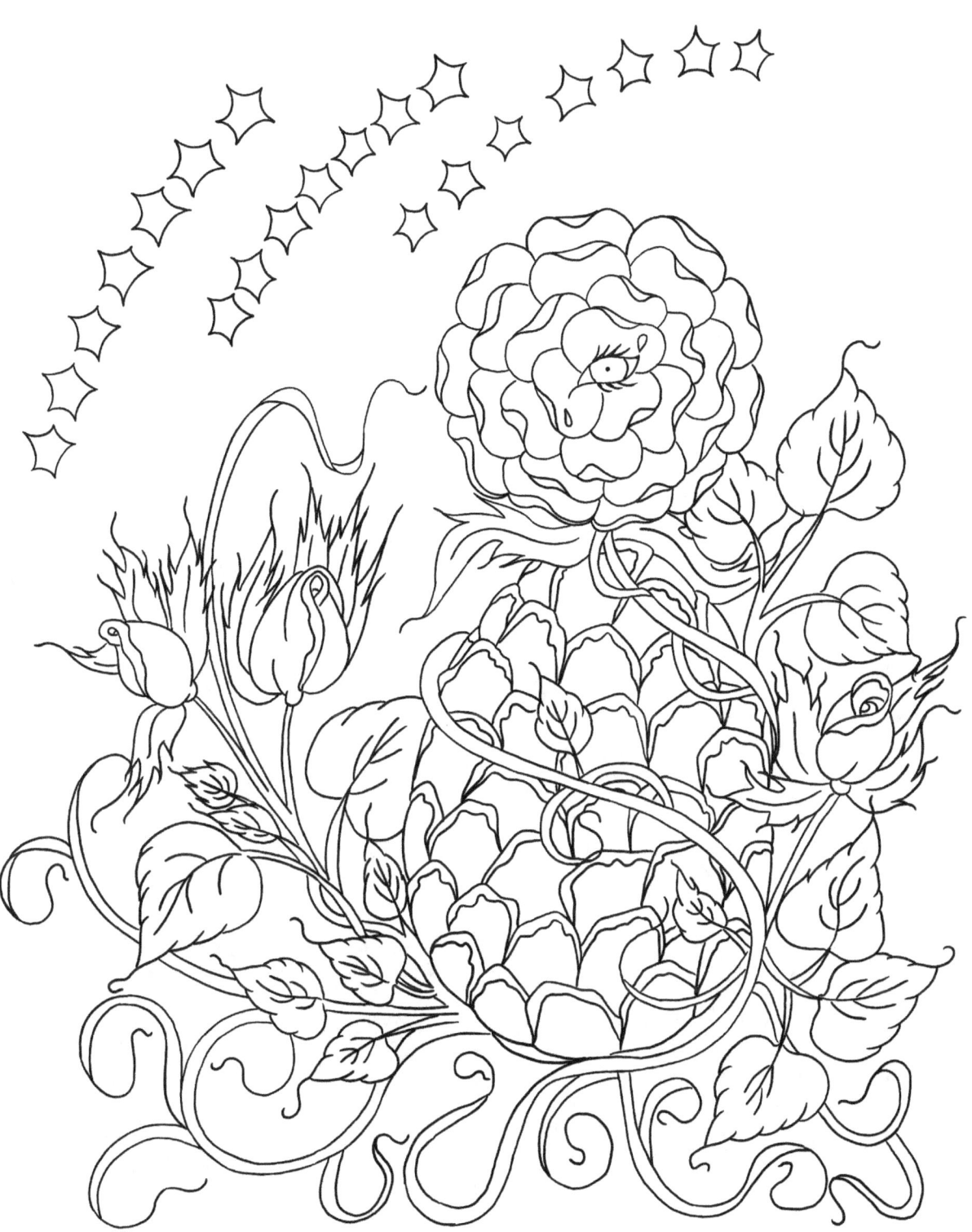

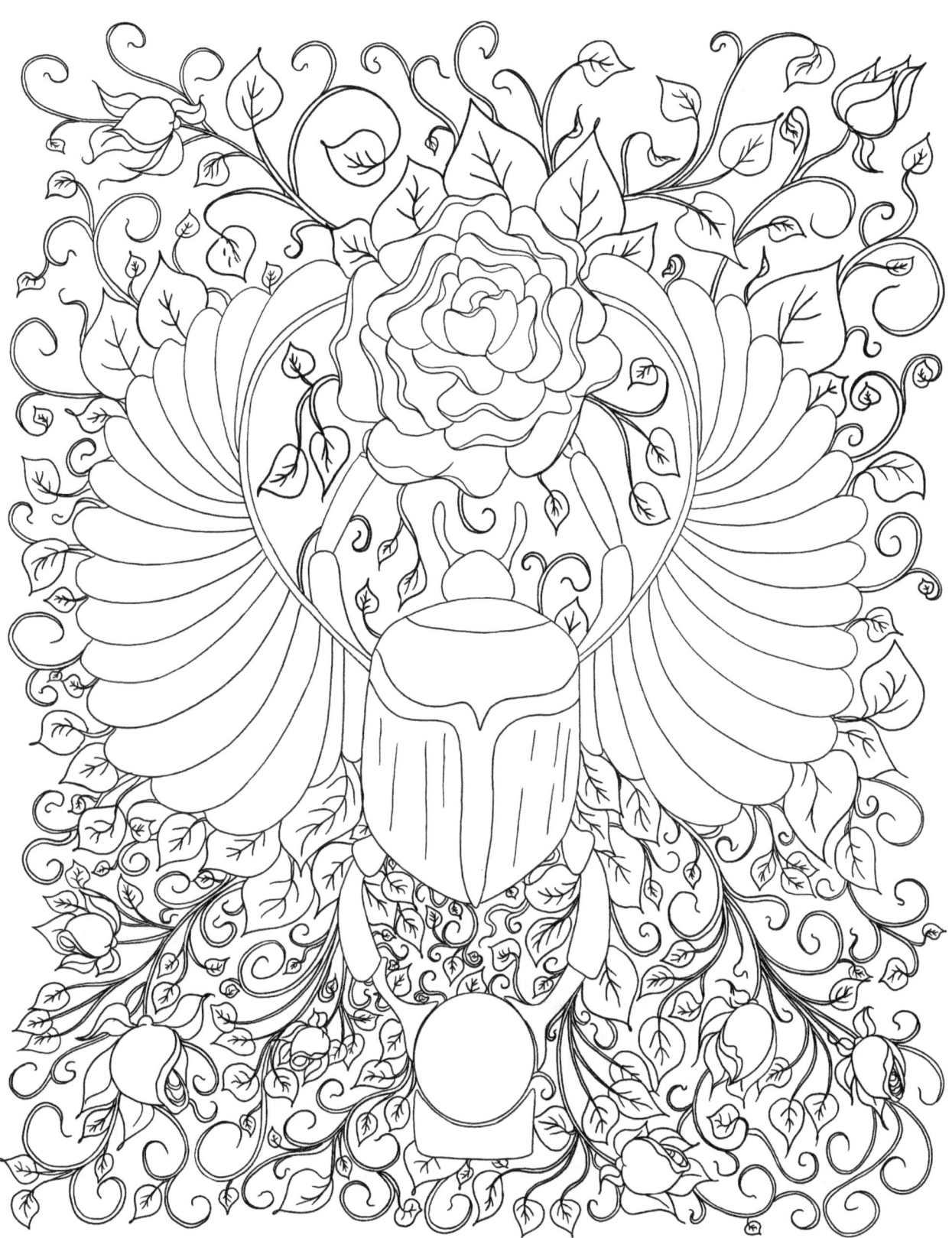

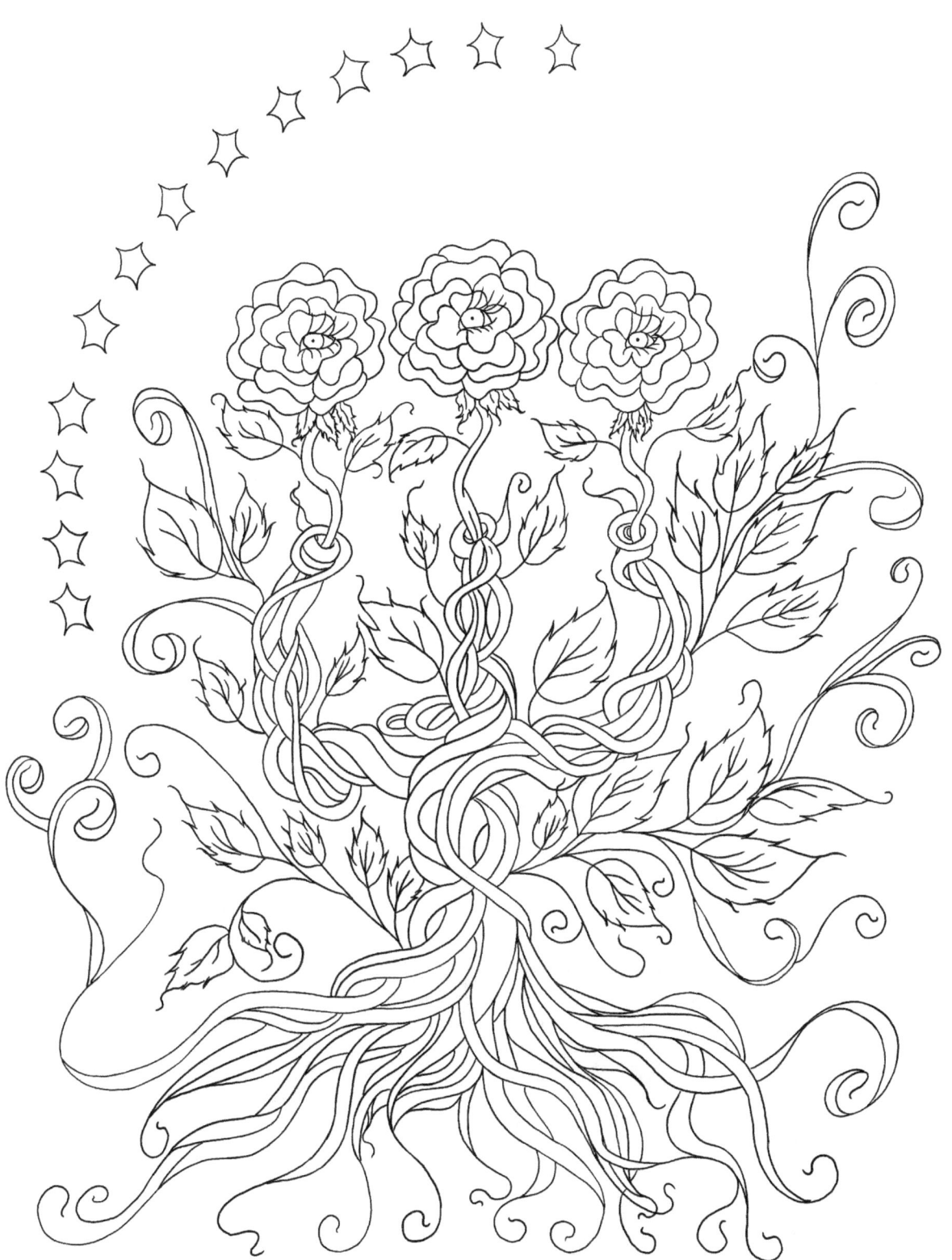

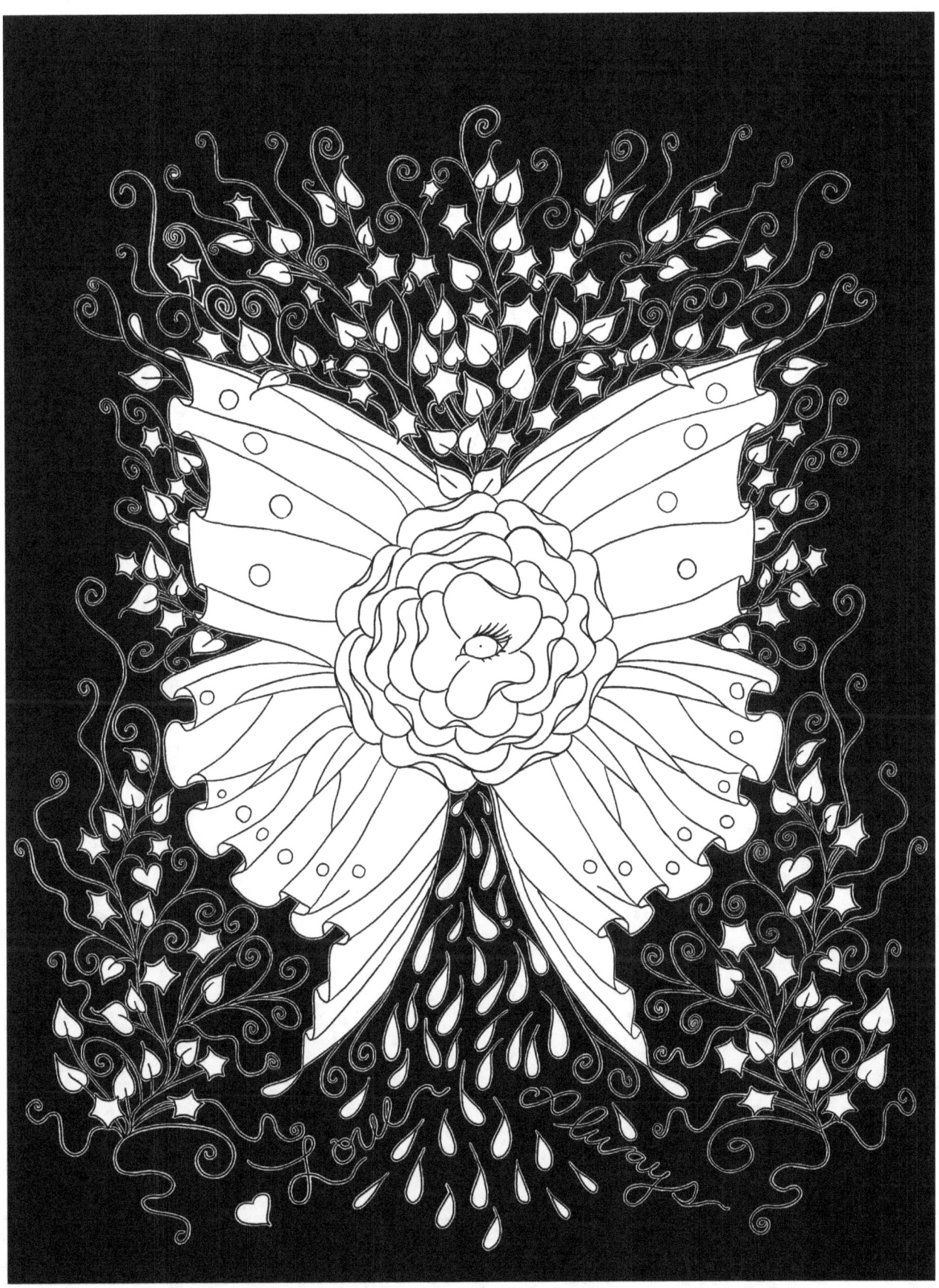

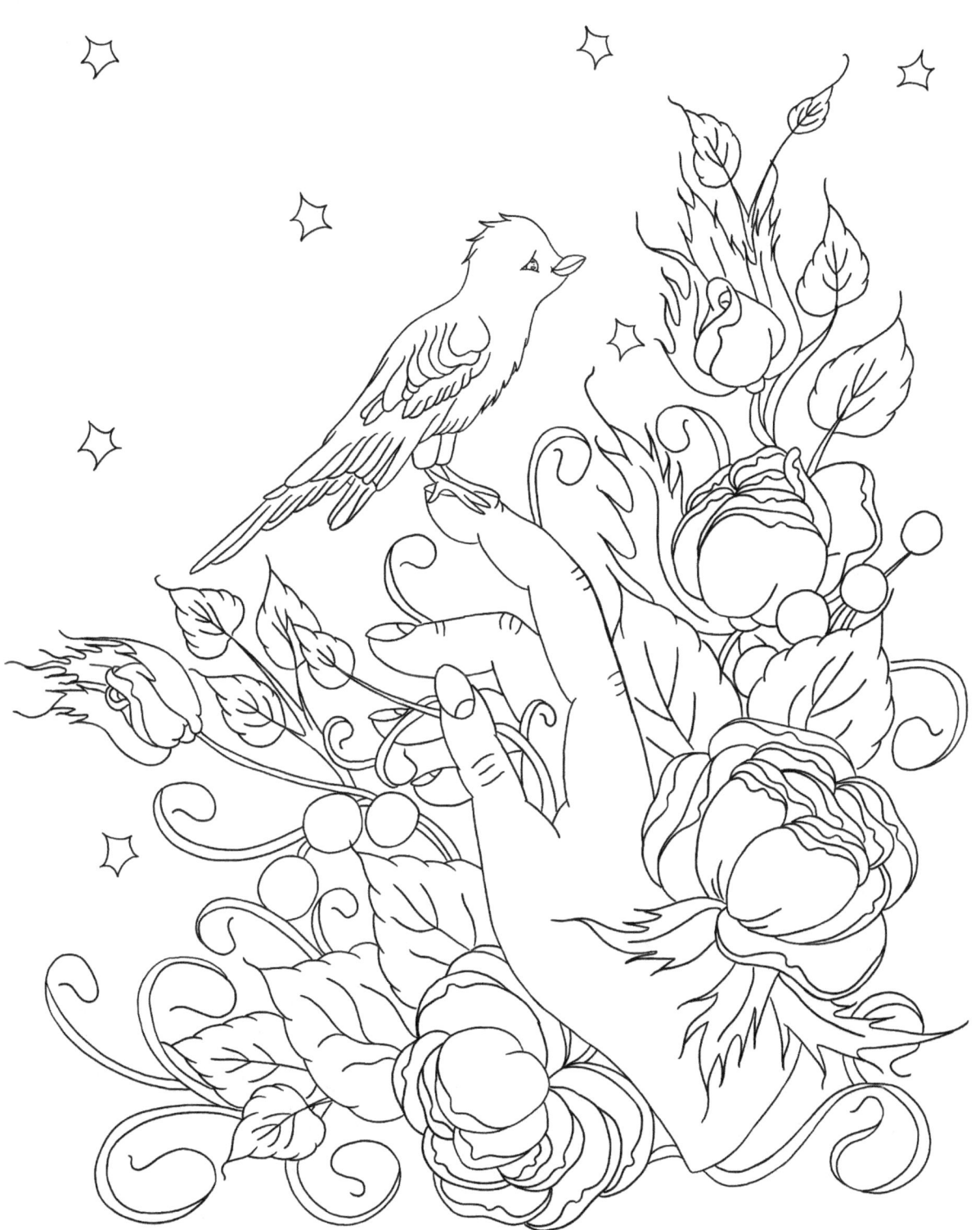

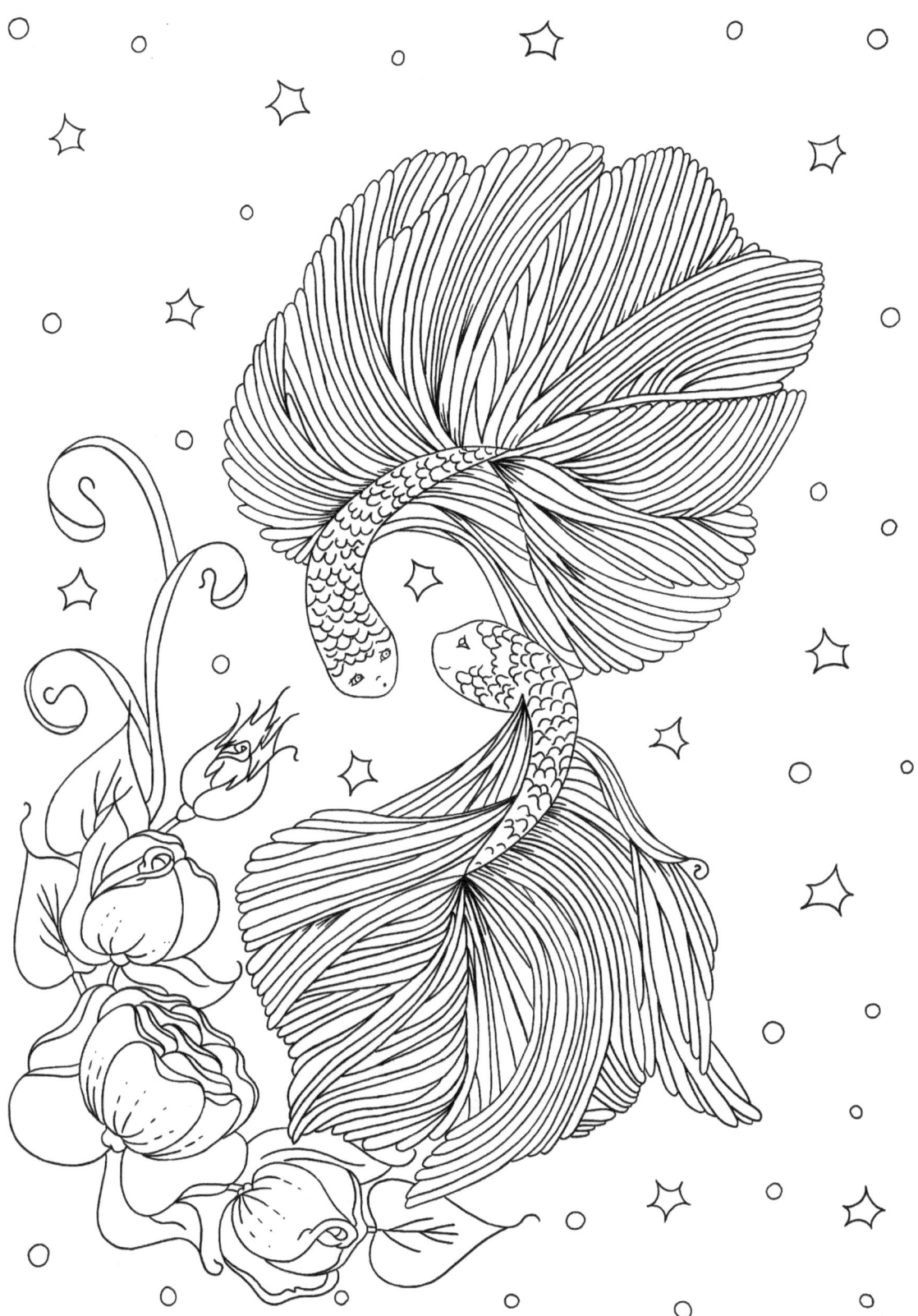

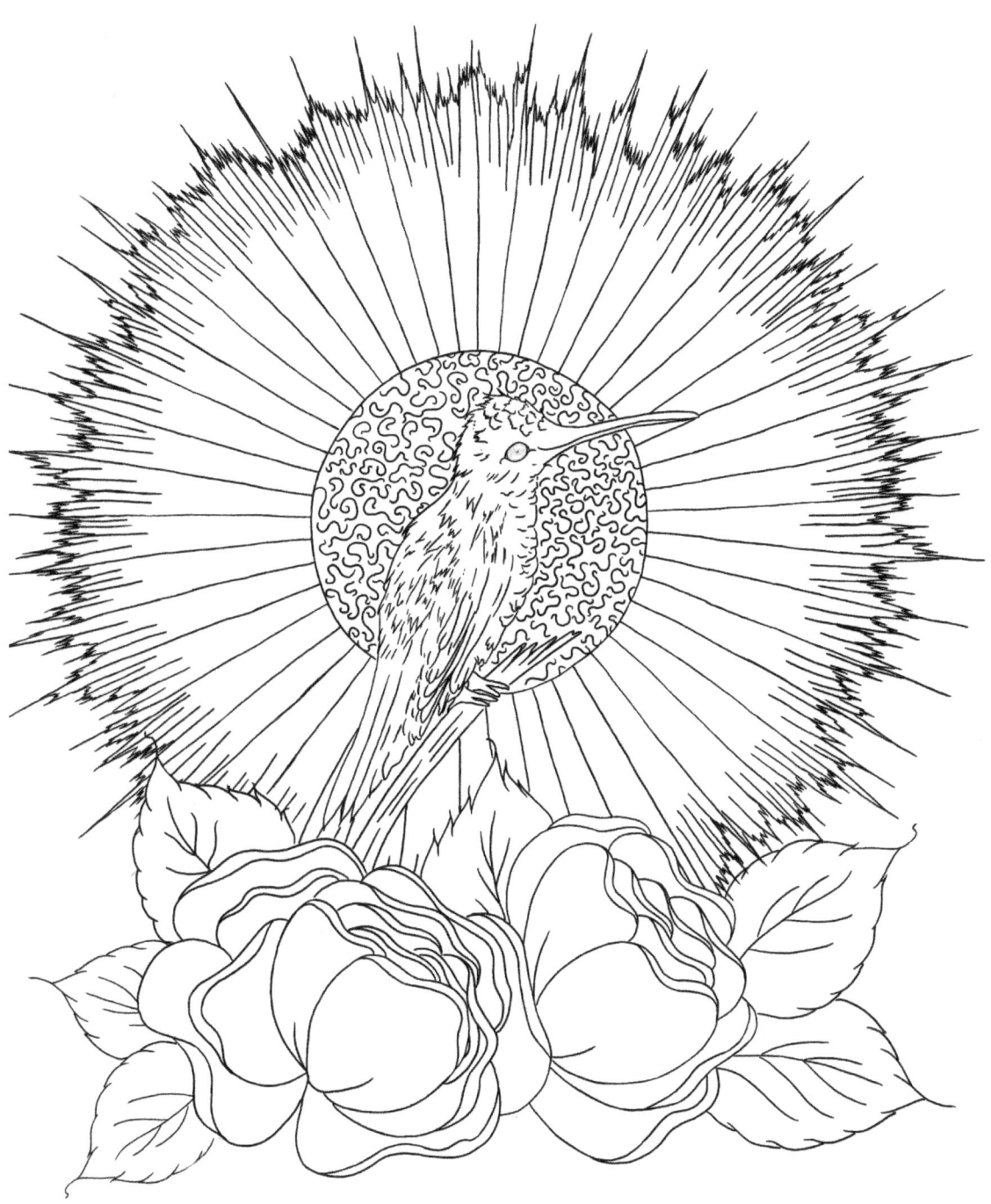

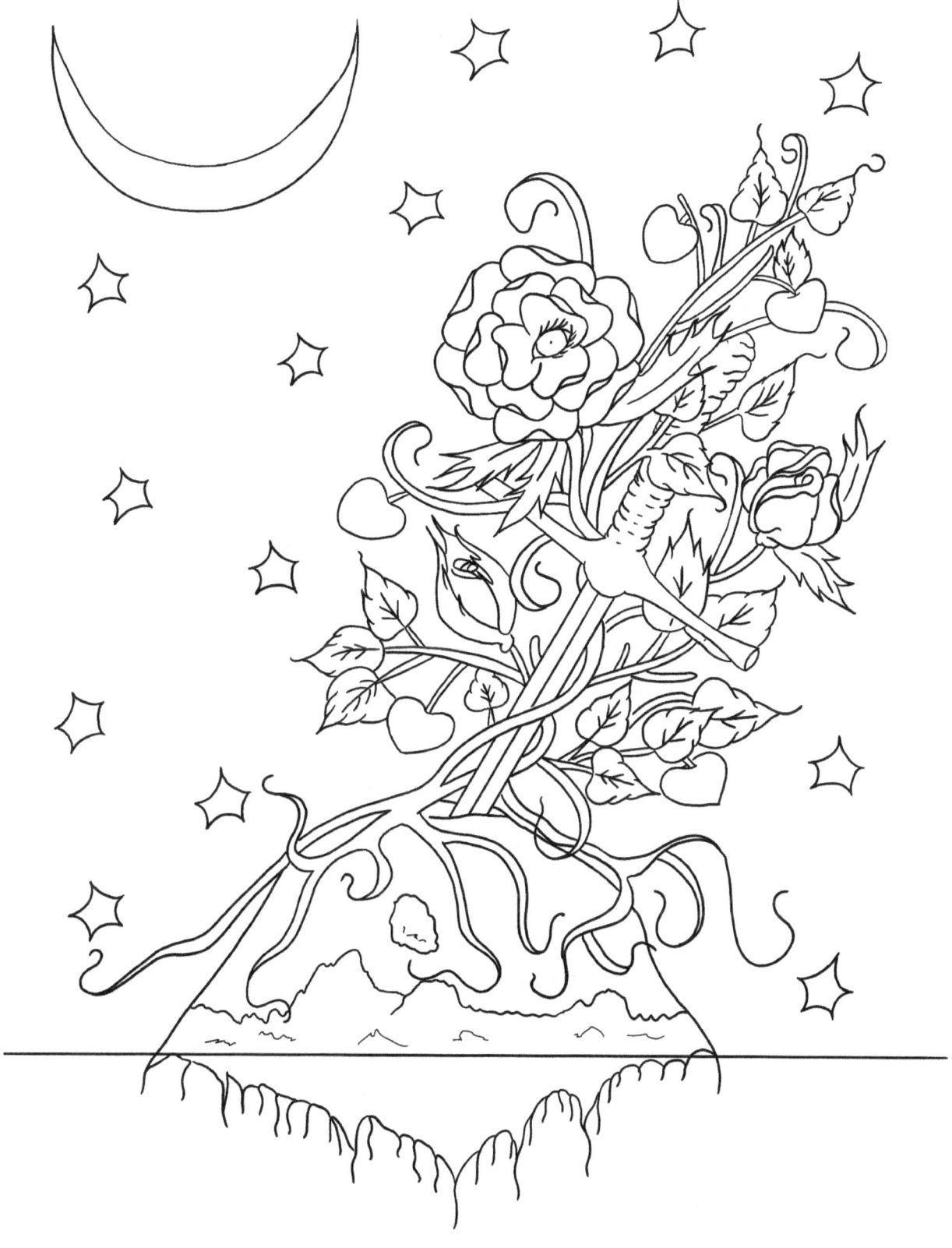

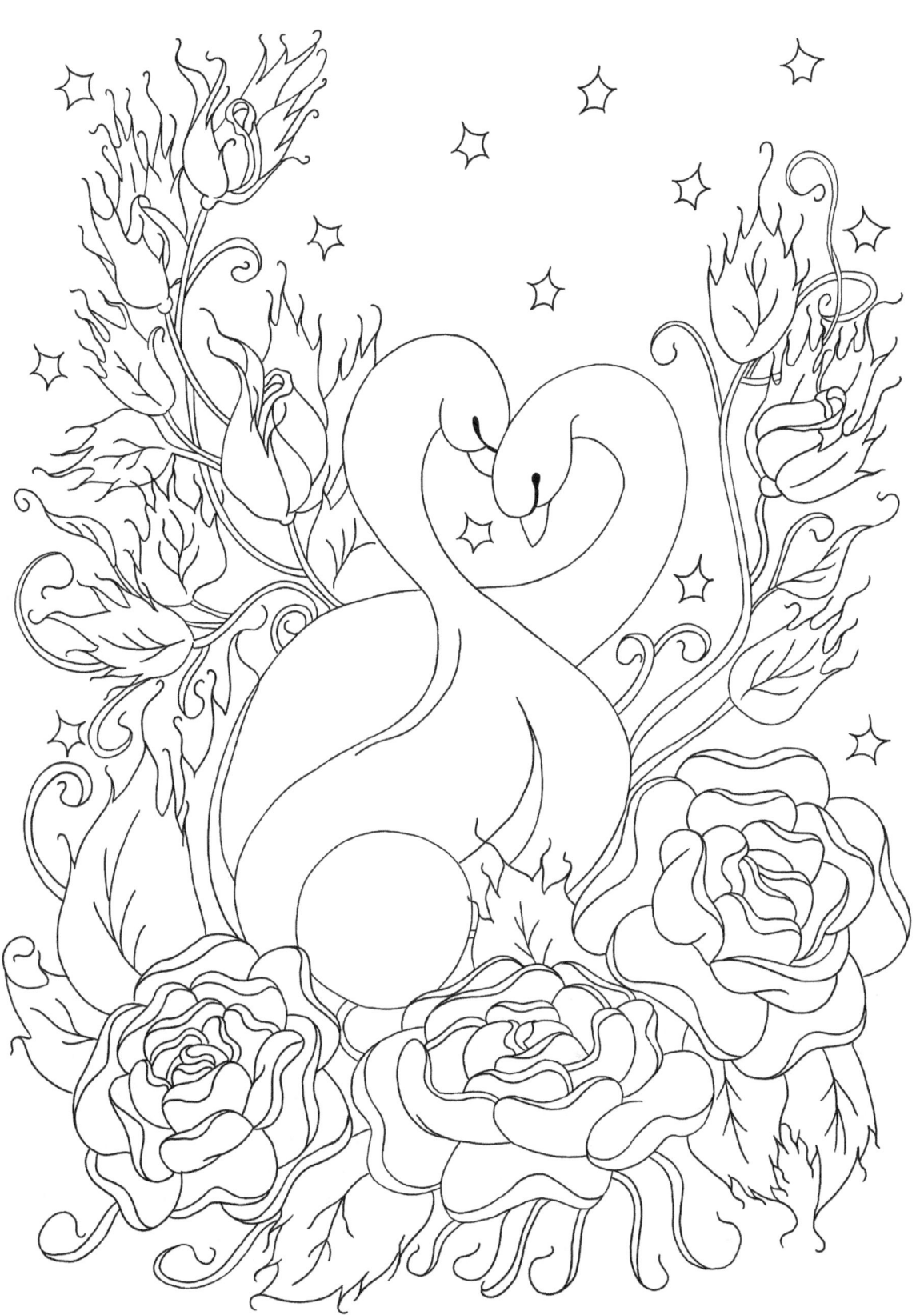

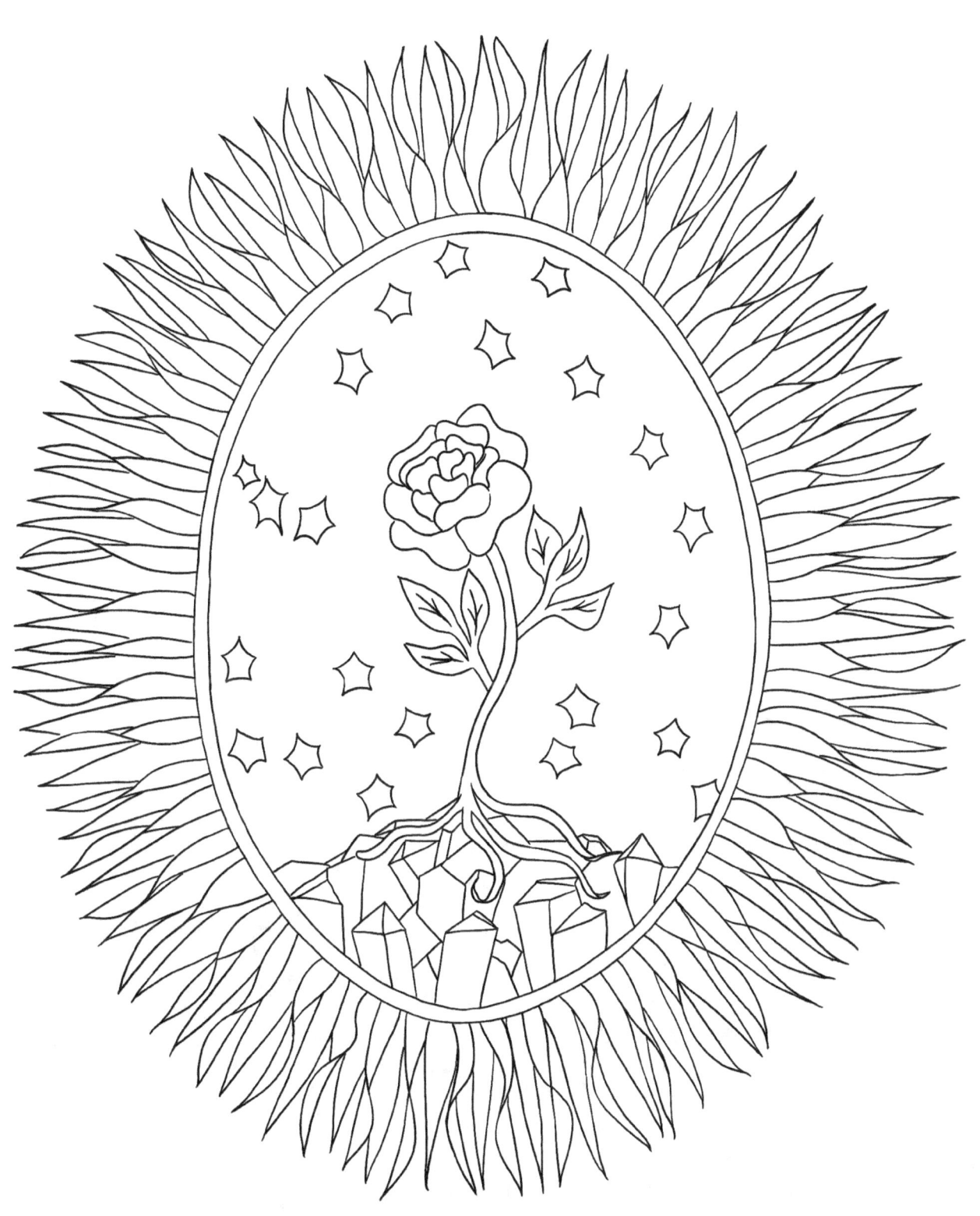

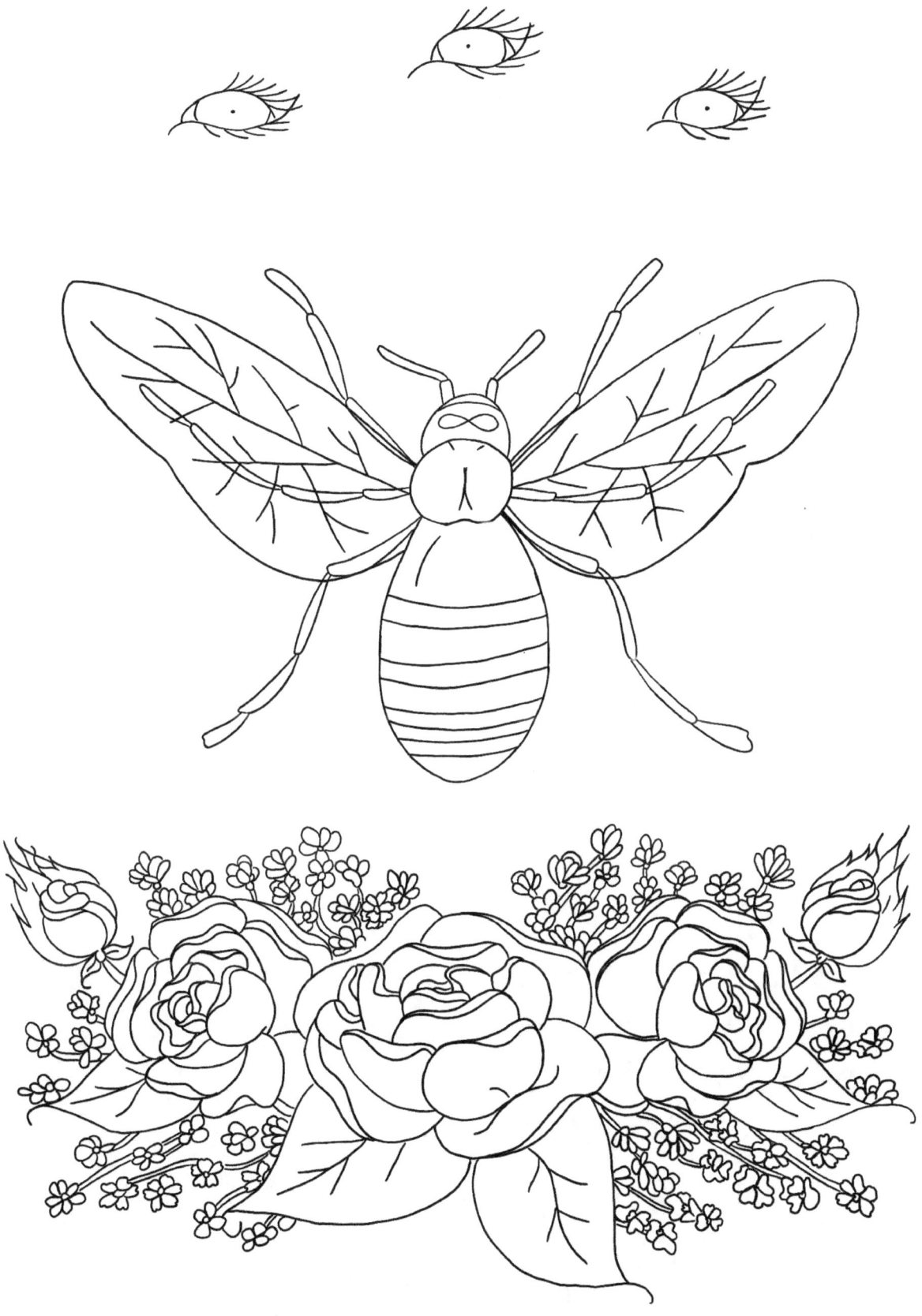

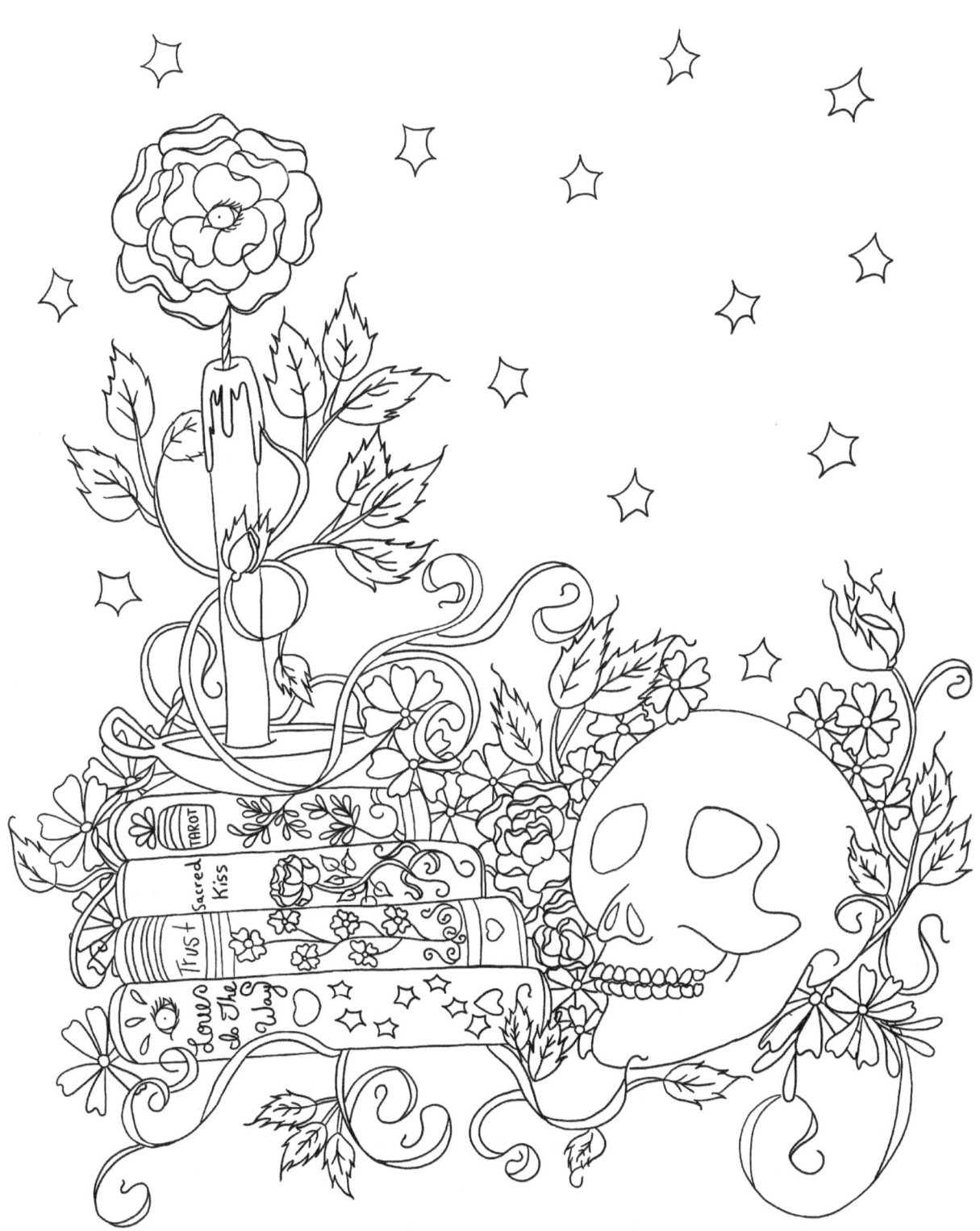

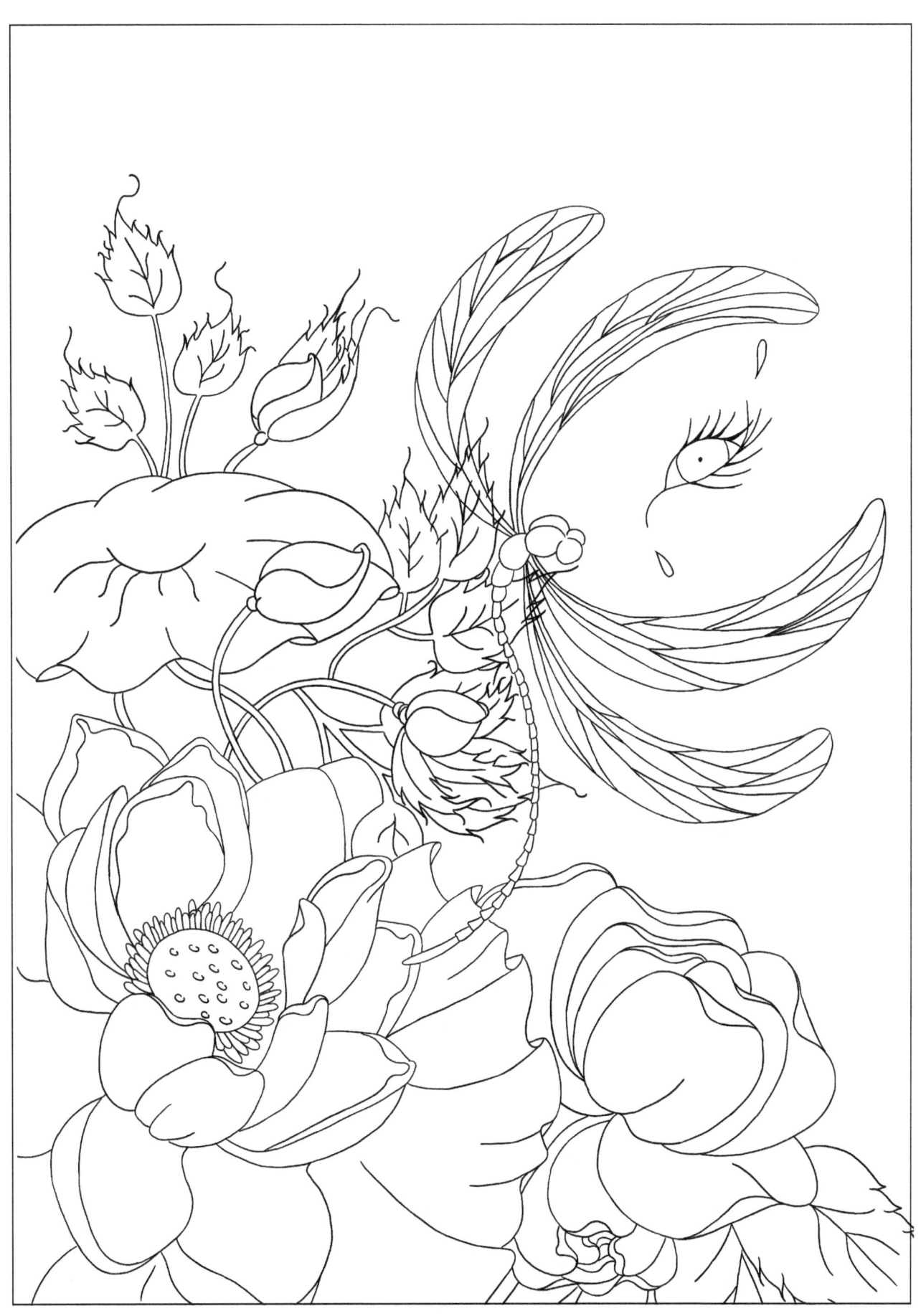

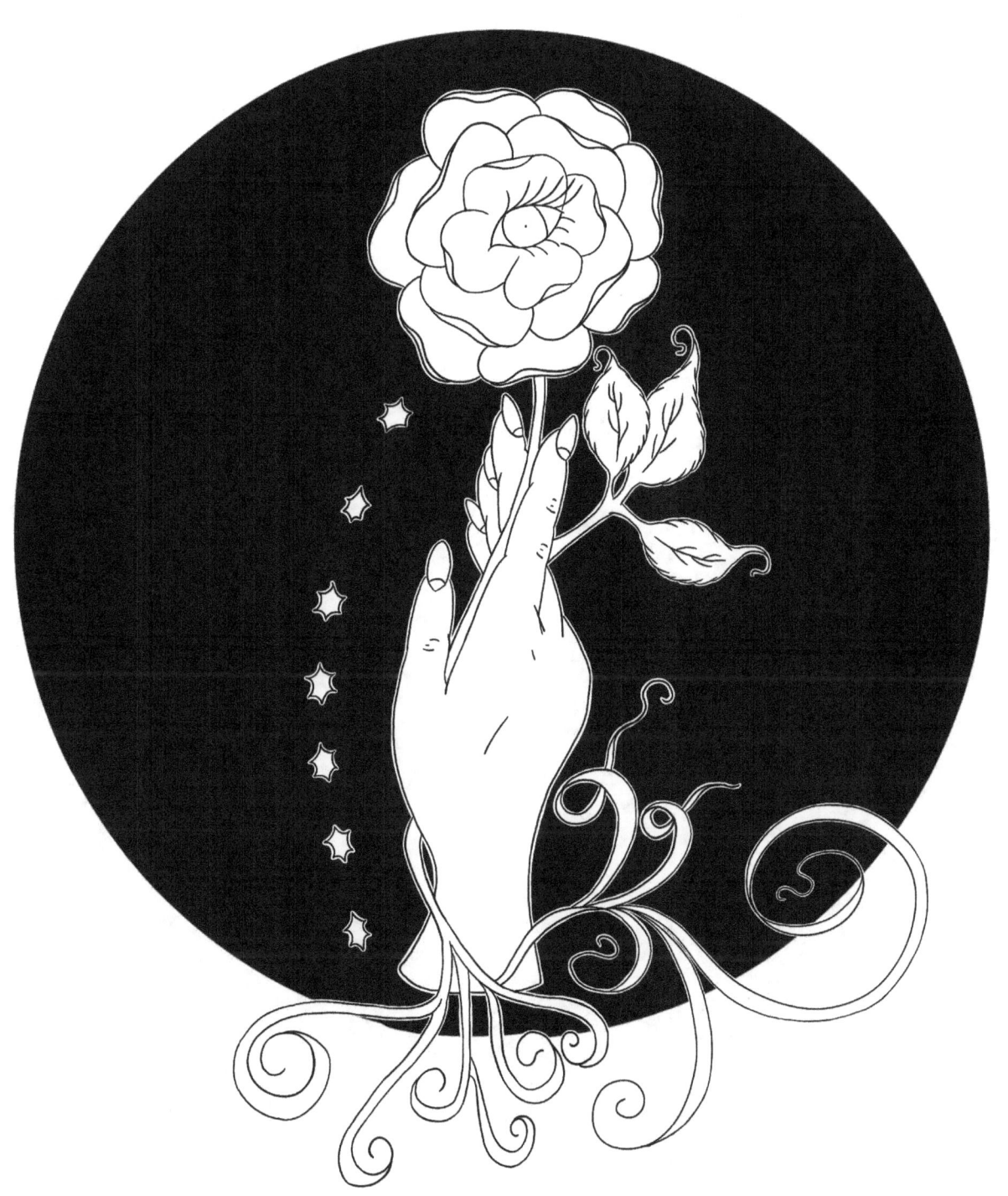

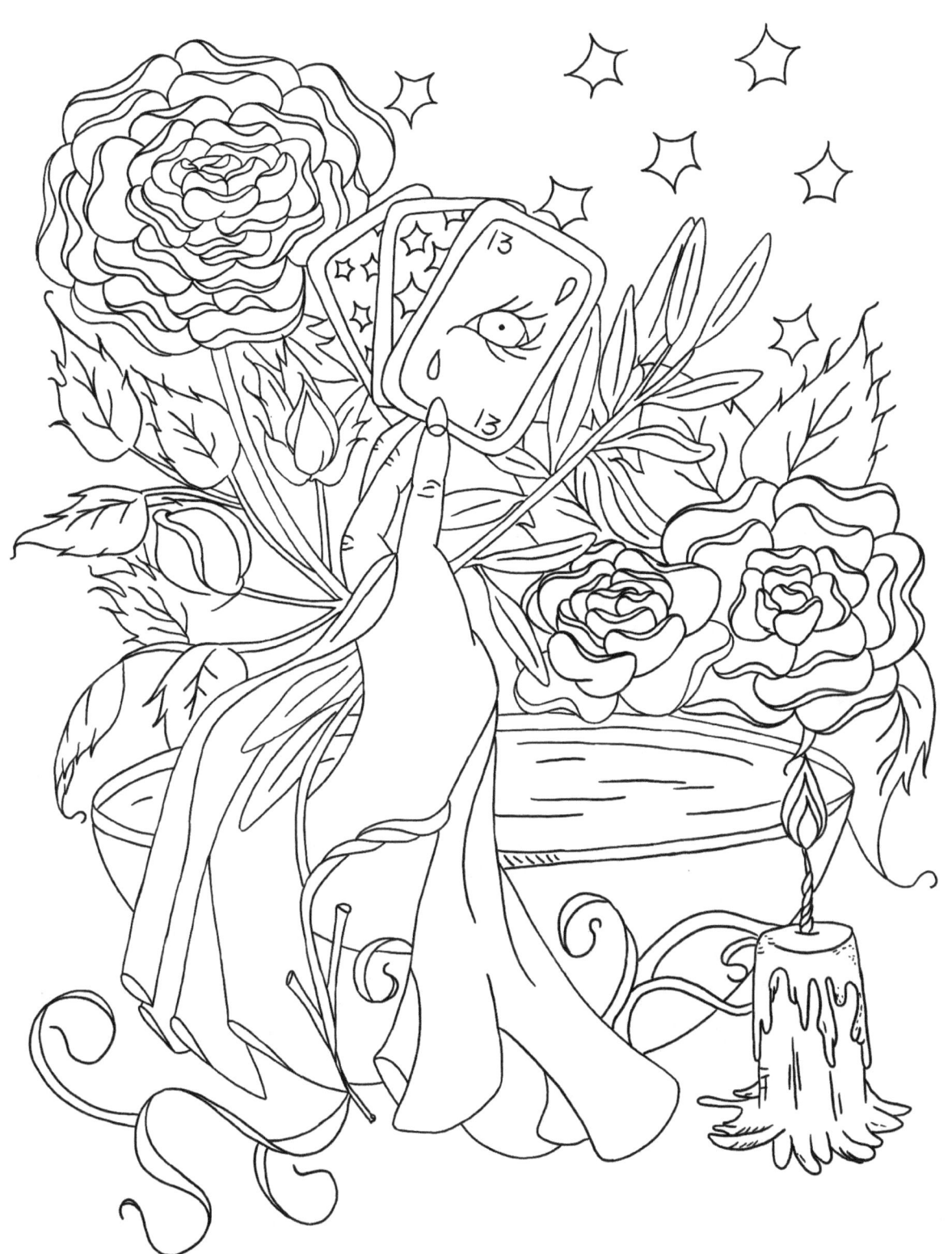

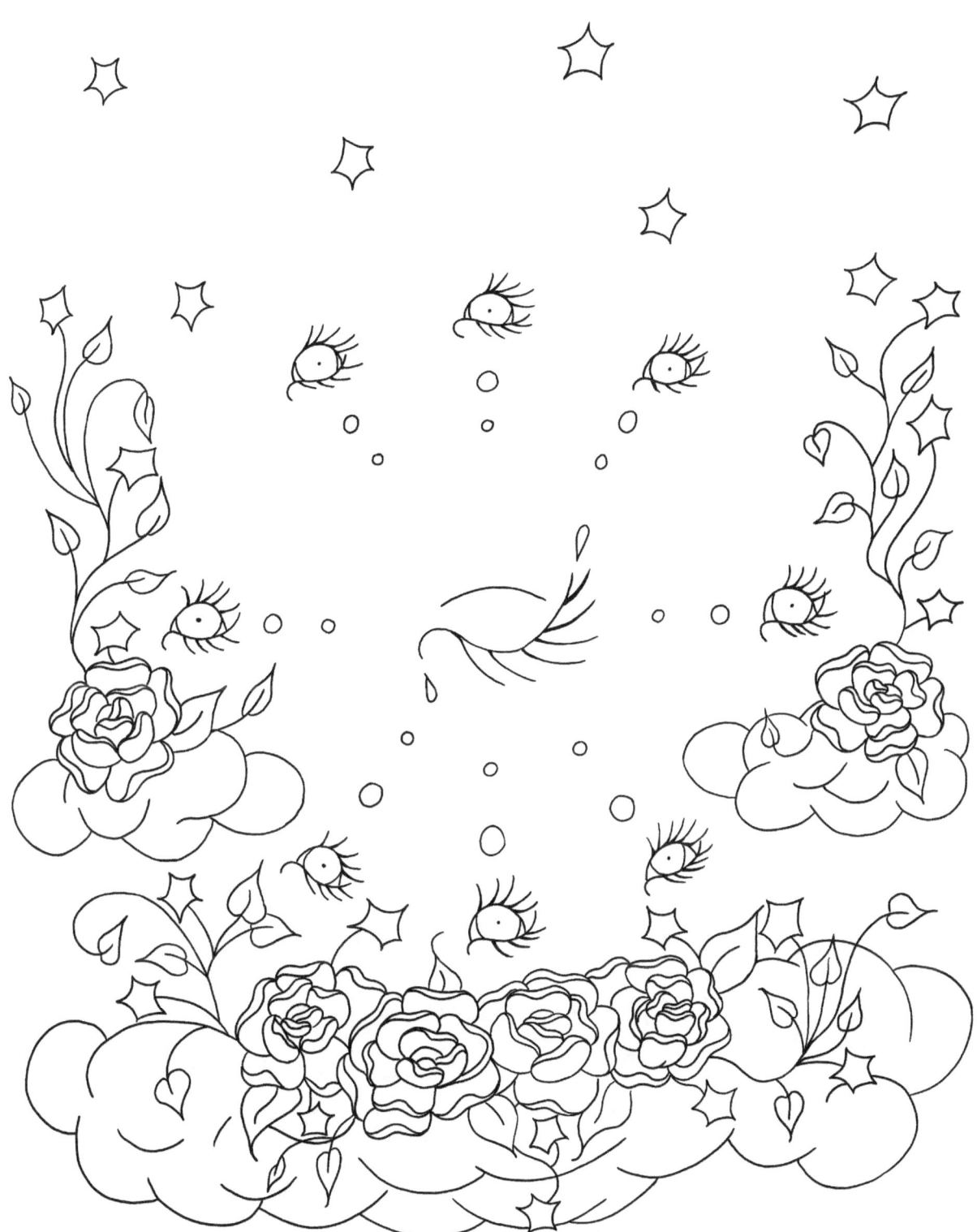

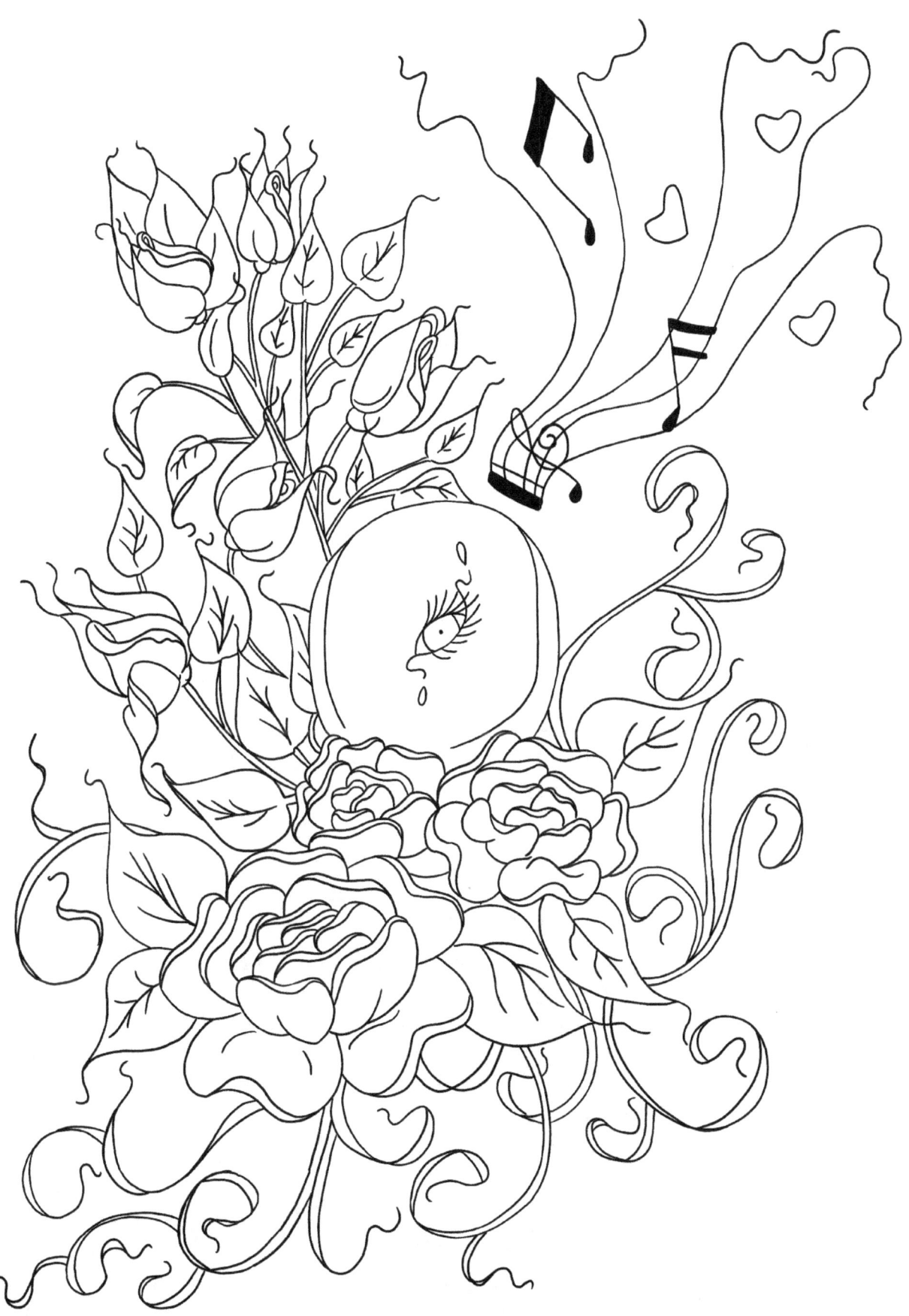

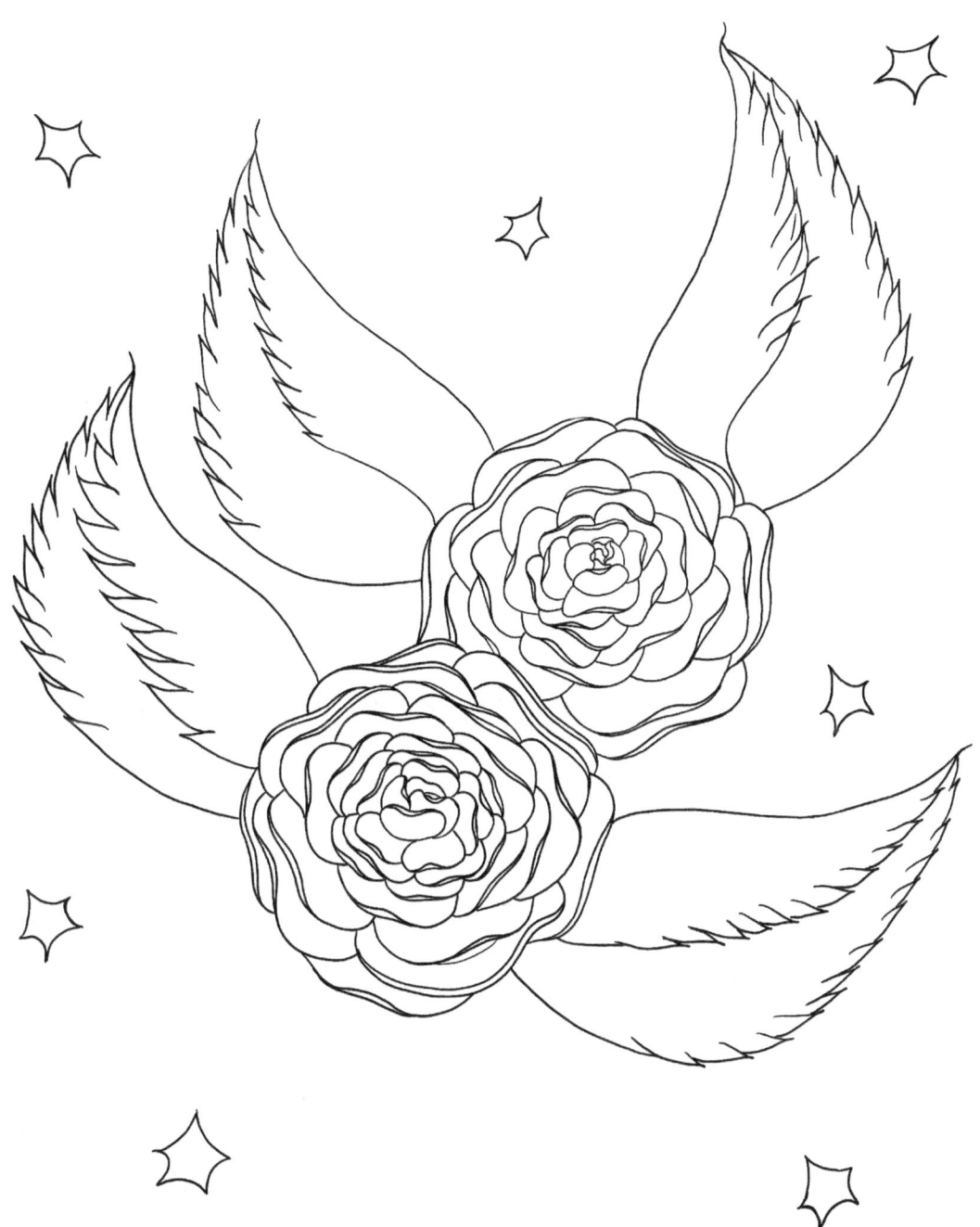

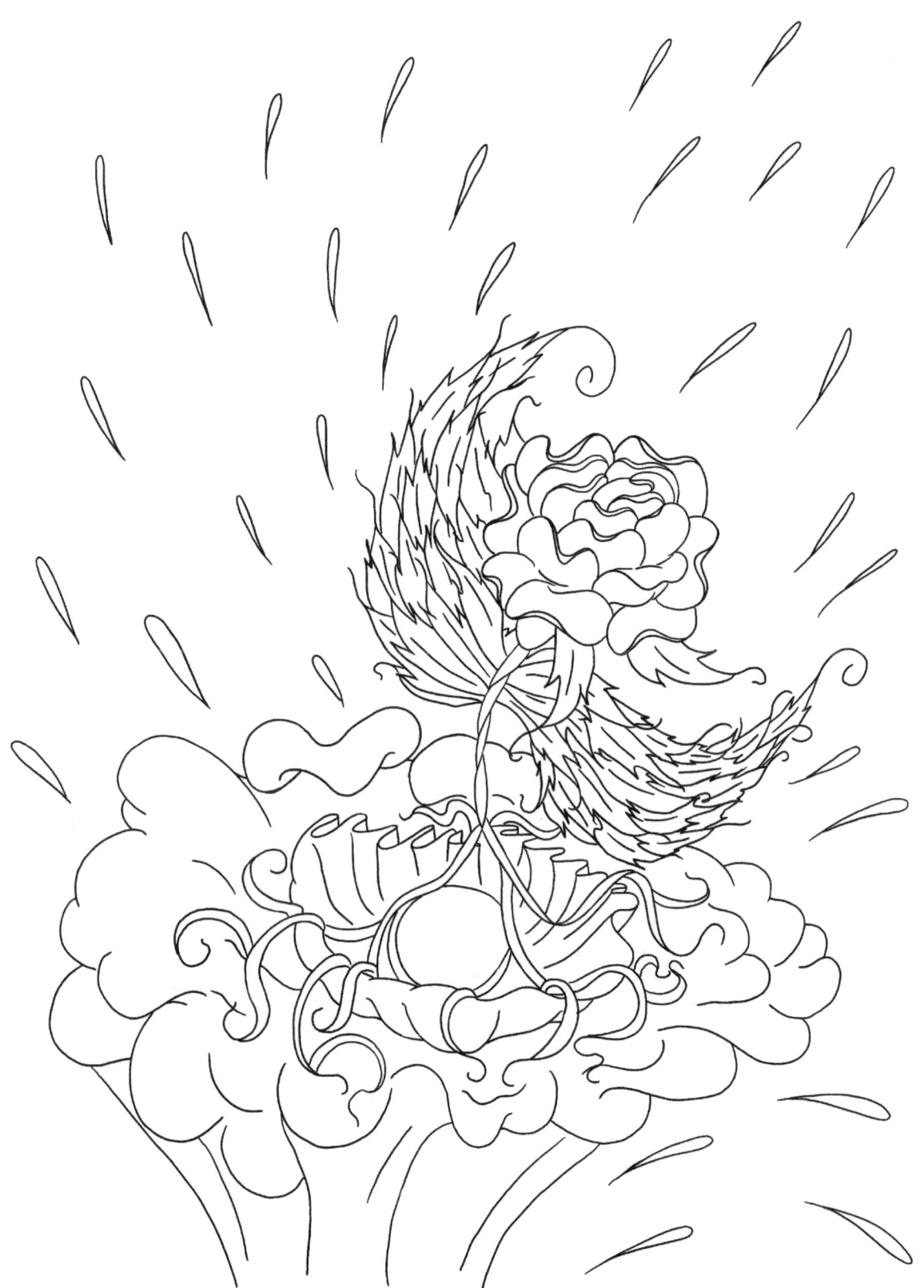

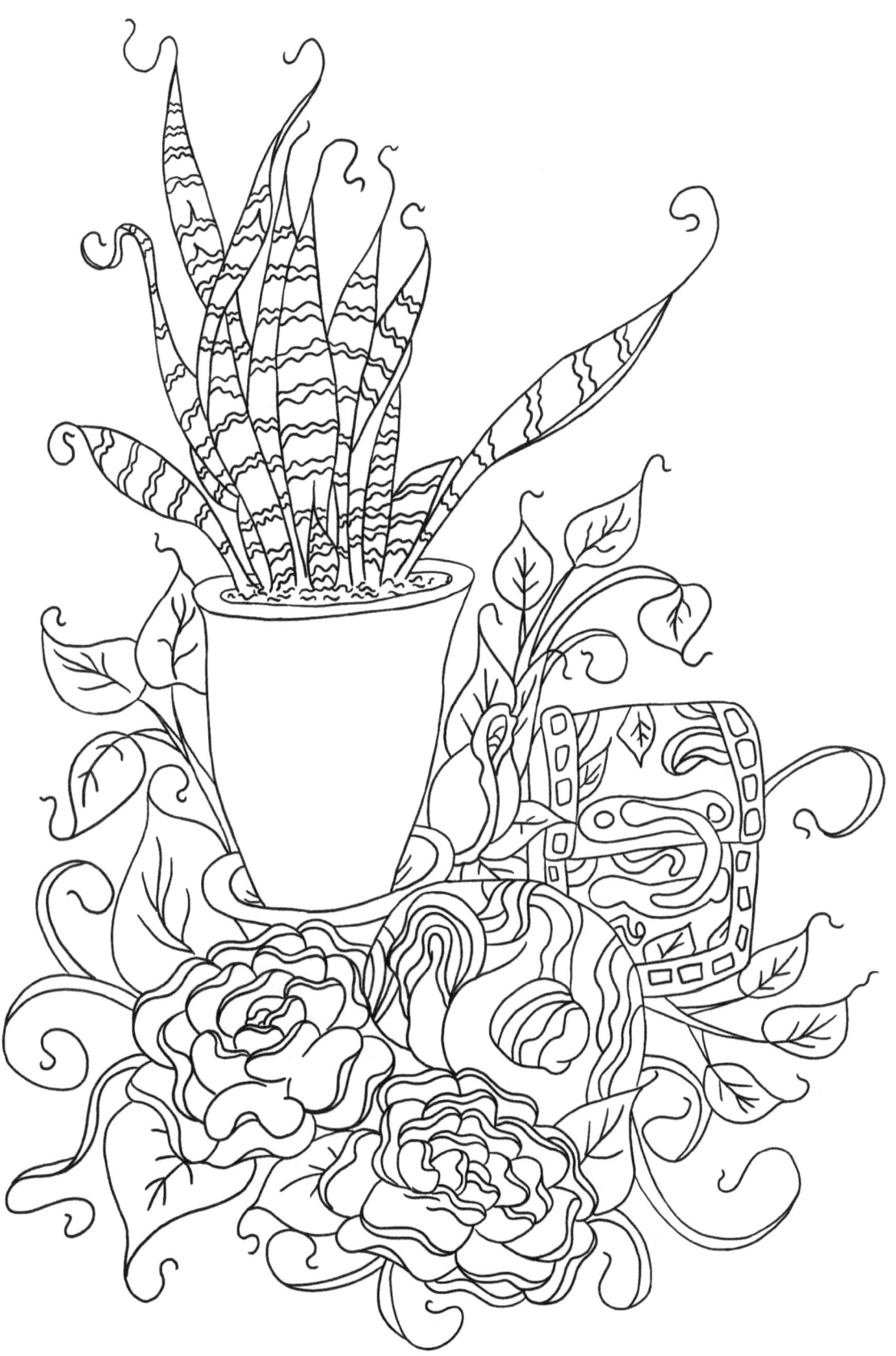

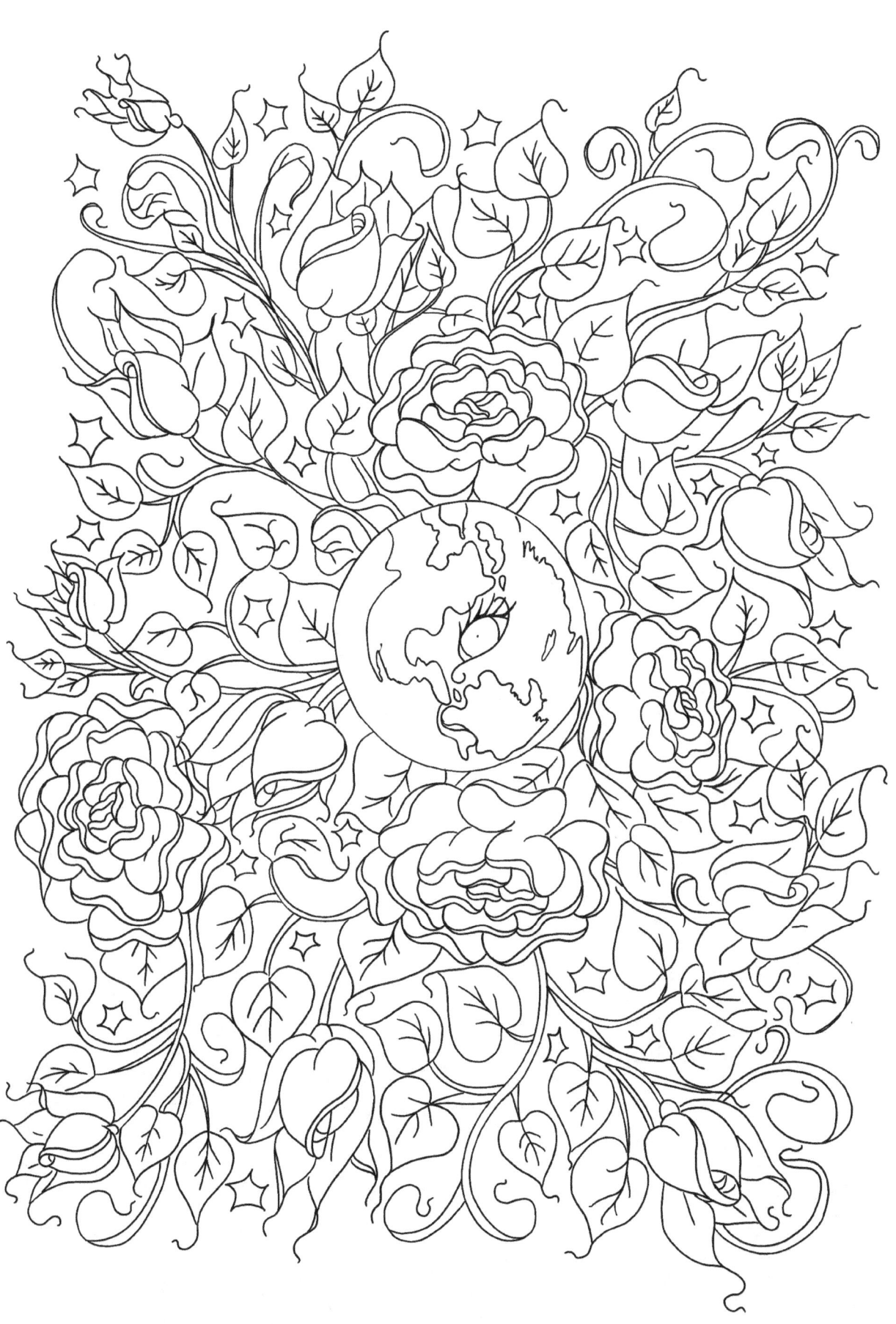

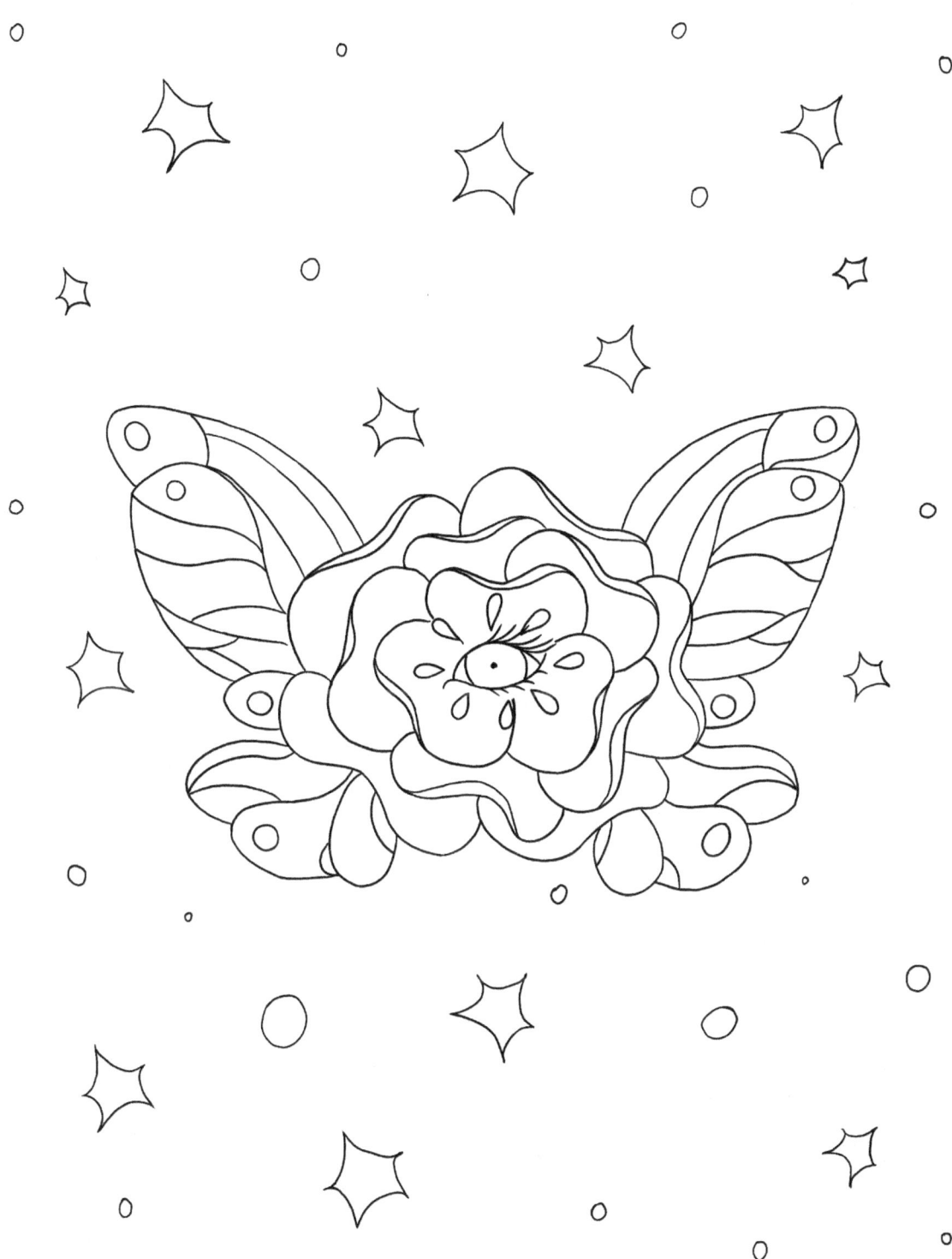

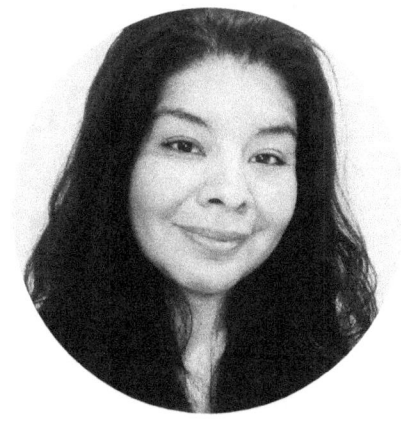

Bringing Back The Substance Of Love To Our Reality

About The Artist

Isis Escobar Salcedo is a visionary artist who creates art inspired in her dreams, spiritual visions, and comprehensions given to her heart through her inner gnosis.

She shares her spiritual knowledge through her art, art products, classes, and loving creativity.

Learn More About Isis,

www.mybelovedatelier.com

My Beloved Atelier

Thank You